Foreword

I want to extend my deepest thanks to my father. His support and wisdom have greatly influenced my journey, and without him, this book would not exist.

I also want to thank my fellow doctors. Your shared experiences and insights have helped shape the ideas in this book. We've all faced similar challenges, and it's through our shared efforts that I've learned so much.

There was a time when I struggled with managing my finances, just like many of you. I remember lying awake at night, worried about bills and the future. It was a difficult period, but it led me to seek out knowledge and solutions that eventually turned my financial life around. This journey inspired me to write this book and share what I've learned.

This book is written to help other doctors achieve financial freedom. Many of us struggle with managing money and planning for the future. The lessons and strategies in this book have helped many doctors improve their financial situations, allowing them to focus on what they love without worrying about money.

"An investment in knowledge pays the best interest." - Benjamin Franklin. This quote perfectly captures the essence of what I hope to convey. Understanding and managing your finances is one of the best investments you can make for your future.

"Do not save what is left after spending, but spend what is left after saving." - Warren Buffett. This principle is a cornerstone of financial planning and is emphasized throughout this book.

I hope this book will be a helpful guide for you on your path to financial security and success. Remember, every step you take towards understanding and managing your finances is a step towards a more secure and fulfilling life. Don't be discouraged by the challenges—embrace them as opportunities to learn and grow.

Thank you for allowing me to be a part of your journey. Now, let's get started on the road to financial freedom.

With gratitude,

Amir Baluch

Table of Contents

Prelude: The Awakening 7

The Pricey Path to MD 9

The Late Starter's Hustle 9

Getting Schooled in Money Matters 9

Introduction: From Trials to Triumph 10

Act I: The Awakening of Wealth 10

Chapter 1: Discovering Your Financial Pulse 10

   1.1 The Debt Dilemma 12

      The Real Deal on Debt 12

      Strategies to Knock It Down 12

      Winning the Mental Game 13

   1.2 Defining Financial Goals 14

      Dream Big, Start Small 14

      Know Your Why 15

      Track, Tweak, Triumph 17

   1.3 Cultivating Financial Confidence 20

      Starting Small: Baby Steps to Big Wins 20

      Knowledge is Power: Learning to Love the Lingo 22

      Following Mistakes: The Stepping Stones to Success 23

      Learning on the Go 23

      Building Your Safety Net 23

      Celebrate Each Step Forward 24

      Next Up: Making Your Money Work 24

Case Study 26

Case Study 1: Dr. Emily's Budgeting Breakthrough 26

Case Study 2: Dr. Jordan's Investment Journey 26

Case Study 3: Dr. Brett Learning Curve 27

Chapter 2: The Wealth Mindset 28

2.1 Overcoming Traditional Constraints 29

2.2 Escaping Lifestyle Creep 32

    Budgeting Like a Boss 32

    The Joy of Saying "No" 34

    Investing in Experiences, Not Things 35

2.3 Follow Risk and Reward Asymmetric Returns 37

    Finding Your Risk Comfort Zone 37

    Balancing Act: Diversification and Allocation 38

    Follow the Long Game 40

Chapter 3: The Alchemy of Money 42

3.1 Maximizing Investment Opportunities 42

    "An investment in knowledge pays the best interest." 45

    – Benjamin Franklin 45

3.2 Strategic Debt Management 47

3.3 The Power of Compound Interest 51

Act II: Mastering the Art of Wealth 54

Chapter 4: Strategic Wealth Design 54

4.1 Designing a Diversified Portfolio 55

4.2 Investment Strategies for the Busy Doctor 58

    Auto-Pilot Investing 58

    Becoming a Limited Partner in a Syndication or Fund 59

Benefits of Being a Limited Partner 61

Time Blocking for Financial Check-Ins 62

4.3 Navigating Market Fluctuations 64

Sticking Through the Ups and Downs 64

Keeping Cool When It Heats Up 65

Staying the Course 65

Chapter 5: Diversifying Your Income Canvas 67

5.1 Exploring Side Hustles 68

5.2 Passive Income Streams for Physicians 70

5.3 Balancing Medicine and Entrepreneurship 72

Setting Boundaries for Work and Play 72

Smart Time Management Strategies 72

Leveraging Your Network 73

Following Flexibility and Adaptability 73

Maintaining Work-Life Harmony 73

Side Hustles 74

Passive Income Streams 75

Chapter 6: The Fortress of Financial Solitude 77

6.1 The Essentials of Disability Insurance 79

6.2 Protecting Your Assets 82

Understanding Liability Coverage 82

Strategic Asset Ownership 82

Incorporating Your Practice 83

6.3 Estate Planning for Physicians 85

Dr. Smith's Trust Fund Triumph 86

Dr. Jones and the Guardianship Game-Changer 87

The Unexpected Tax Tackle by Dr. Patel 87
Dr. Lee's Legacy Locked In 87
Dr. Garcia's Guardianship Go-To 87

Chapter 7: The Art of Tax Efficiency 89

7.1 Tax Planning for High Earners 90
Advanced Strategies for High-Income Docs 90
Smart Income Timing 90
Utilizing Tax-Deferred Accounts 91
Strategic Asset Location 92

7.2 Understanding Tax-Advantaged Accounts 94

7.3 Tax-Efficient Investing 96
Choosing the Right Account for the Right Investment 96
Smart Moves with Mutual Funds 98
The Beauty of Tax-Loss Harvesting 99
Here are some practical approaches and case studies drawn from experts in the field: 100

Conclusion: Mastering the Tax Game 103

Chapter 8: Envisioning Early Retirement 104

8.1 Calculating Retirement Needs 105
Understanding Your Lifestyle Choices 105
Inflation's Impact 106
Future Healthcare Needs 106

8.2 The Path to Financial Independence 108
Following Diverse Income Streams 108
Investing Wisely 109
Mastering Money Management 111

8.3 Sustainable Withdrawal Strategies 113
Flexibility Is Key 113
The Bucket Strategy 115
Conclusion: Setting Sail for Early Retirement 116

Chapter 9: Leaving a Legacy 117
9.1 Philanthropy as a Legacy 118
The Ripple Effect of Giving 118
Building a Philanthropic Strategy 119
Legacy Through Philanthropy 119
9.2 Structuring a Lasting Legacy 121
9.3 Family and Financial Education 123
Conclusion 125
Epilogue: The Renaissance Never Ends 126
Continued Learning and Growth 126
The Community of Financially Savvy Physicians 126
Appendices: The Renaissance Toolkit 127
Resources for Financial Education 127
Tools for Financial Management 127

Prelude: The Awakening

I'm a failure.

At 21, my life took a tough turn. I didn't get into medical school, and the same year, my dad, a doctor, lost all his money. We had to sell almost everything we owned and move into a tiny apartment that cost us $250 a month. It was a big change for us, especially since my dad used to earn a lot.

Lying there on my air mattress, looking up at the ceiling fan, I learned something important: you can't just depend on one way to make money. My dad worked hard, but he didn't spread his risks or plan well enough. That's why things went so wrong for us.

When I got the letter saying I didn't get into med school, I didn't let it stop me. I decided to gain knowledge, not just about one thing, but about lots of different ways to handle money and business.

I was lucky to meet some great people who taught me a lot about finance. They helped me see opportunities I never knew existed. I got to share what I learned with others through articles and news sites like Forbes and Yahoo! Finance. After I got rejected from med school, I didn't let it stop me. I wanted to learn from the best, so I got my securities license and spent the next five years at a boutique investment bank and broker-dealer. I worked on big projects, totaling over $700 million. Later, I used that experience to help large companies manage their finances better. I learned something new with each project and from every doctor and professional that I met.

I'm Amir, a doc who shifted to part-time work with the stethoscope in my early 40s. Now, I'm here to share how you can find a similar balance. It's about blending the fulfillment of medicine with the financial freedom of other ventures—like swapping war stories but with less blood and more bucks.

I don't want to gatekeeper all that I learned through these tough times I faced. Instead, I want to help 10,000 people like you find ways to make money without having to work all the time. I want to share the lessons from those hard days and the smart moves I made in business. My goal is to help you get to a place where you're comfortable with your money, faster than you thought possible.

My story shows that things don't always go as planned. But it's in those tough times that we learn the most. I'm here to guide you in making smart money choices, so you can live the life you want, sooner than you think.

Every chapter in this book holds lessons that can guide you toward financial freedom. Don't skip any chapters, as each one contains hidden gems that could forever transform your life. As you come to the end of this book, remember: Your financial future begins with the choices you make today. Apply the knowledge you've gained to make wise decisions. The power to rewrite your financial narrative and turn your dreams into reality is in your hands.

"If you don't find a way to make money while you sleep, you will work until you die." -Warren Buffett

Scan the QR code below to see my interview by CBS news on physician investment education and my first book:

The Pricey Path to MD

So, you've survived med school and got the fancy degree to prove it. But if you're like many of us, you're also saddled with a hefty $200,000 in student loans. Yep, you heard that right. And while 43% of us are in that boat, only about a third feel ready to tackle that monster debt. It's like starting a marathon with a backpack full of bricks. Not ideal, right?

The Late Starter's Hustle

Here's the deal: we get a late pass to the earning game. When most folks are starting to save and invest, we're still hitting the books or training. But it's not all doom and gloom. Despite kicking off later, we've got the potential to catch up and even zoom past our peers, thanks to our earning power. The trick? Not falling into the trap of spending more as we earn more. Tough, I know, but totally doable.

Getting Schooled in Money Matters

Let's be real: med school taught us how to save lives, not save money. A quarter of us feel like we're playing catch-up on the retirement front. But here's a secret: managing money is a skill, and anyone can learn it. Yes, even you, with your crazy schedule and all.

Introduction: From Trials to Triumph

Act I: The Awakening of Wealth

Chapter 1: Discovering Your Financial Pulse

Hey there! Welcome to Chapter 1, here we'll get up close and personal with your finances. Think of this as the "getting to know you" phase, but instead of awkward small talk, we're diving straight into the good stuff – your financial health.

We're starting with the big, hairy monster under the bed – med school debt. Yep, it's a doozy, with the average doc carrying around $200,000 in student loans. Feels like a mountain, right? But don't sweat it; we're going to tackle this together.

Next up, we're setting some goals. And not just any goals – the kind that makes you jump out of bed in the morning.

"Considering only 20% of doctors feel they're nailing their retirement plans, it's clear we have significant work ahead of us."

But hey, that's what we're here for.

And finally, we're boosting that financial confidence. Because let's face it, navigating investments can feel like trying to read a map in a foreign language. And with a quarter of doctors feeling shaky about their investment choices, it's high time we change that.

Now you need to take a very important step. Pause and scan this QR code, so you can get access to a bonus downloadable guide custom-made for you. It is an interactive financial workbook planner as a bonus to this book.

Scan here. To get immediate access.

So, buckle up! We're about to turn that financial pulse from a faint flutter to a strong, steady beat. Ready to dive in? Let's do this!

1.1 The Debt Dilemma

So, we're diving deep into the world of debt, specifically the kind that feels like a mountain on your shoulders right after med school. We're talking a whopping average of $200,000. Yeah, it's a lot, but here's the scoop on how to not just live with it, but tackle it head-on and come out on top.

The Real Deal on Debt

Let's lay it out straight. That big number, $200,000, is what most new docs are up against. It's a hefty sum that can feel like a shadow looming over all your financial moves. But here's a little secret: you're in good company, and there's a way out.

- The thing about interest is that it keeps piling up, kind of like the dishes in your sink. If you're not keeping an eye on it, it can grow from a small pile into a mountain before you know it.

- This debt is in it for the long haul, kind of sticking around like an unwanted guest who decided to move in. It's there when you're having your morning coffee and still there when you're turning off the lights at night.

Strategies to Knock It Down

Now, don't get disheartened. There are some smart moves you can make to chip away at this beast and even save some cash along the way.

- **Refinancing**: Think of this as a do-over for your loan. If you can score a lower interest rate, you're essentially cutting down how much extra you're paying on top of what you borrowed. It's like opting for a lighter backpack before a long hike.

- **Loan Forgiveness:** This one's a bit like finding a hidden treasure map that leads you out of debt. Certain programs will erase some, or all of what you owe if you work in specific areas or fields. It's definitely worth exploring, kind of like finding a shortcut in a maze.

Here's a pro tip: throwing even a little extra cash at your debt regularly can make a big difference. It's like taking small but steady steps on a long journey. Before you know it, you'll look back and see how far you've come.

Winning the Mental Game

- **Debt Isn't a Scarlet Letter:** Got debt? So does nearly every other new doc. It doesn't mean you're bad with money, just that you've made a big investment in your career.

- **Celebrate the Little Victories:** Knocked a bit off your debt? That's a win! Treat it like crossing off days on a prison sentence. Each small payment gets you closer to freedom.

- **Eye on the Prize:** Keep your dream in mind. Whether it's a peaceful retirement or just the joy of a debt-free life, let that vision drive you.

- **Stress Less:** Remember, stress won't shrink your debt. Take a deep breath, focus on what you can control, and keep plugging away. You've tackled med school; you can handle this too.

1.2 Defining Financial Goals

Setting your financial targets isn't just about the numbers; it's about what those numbers mean for your life. Let's break this down into bite-sized pieces, shall we?

Dream Big, Start Small

First thing's first, what's the dream? Maybe it's owning a beach house, being debt-free, or having a hefty nest egg for retirement. Dreams are great, but let's anchor them with some specifics. Think SMART – Specific, Measurable, Achievable, Relevant, Time-bound. Instead of saying, "I want to be rich," how about "I want to save $1 million by 50"? Sounds more like a plan, right?

But here's the truth: 33% of Americans don't have a financial plan because it feels too daunting. The trick? Start small. Break down that million-dollar dream into yearly, monthly, or even daily savings goals. Suddenly, it's not a mountain; it's a series of molehills.

When you've got a big dream, like saving for that dream home or setting up a college fund for the kids, the numbers can feel overwhelming. But here's a little secret: every big achievement starts with a single, small step. It's like eating an elephant—one bite at a time. Not that you'd want to eat an elephant, but you get the idea.

Think about this: if you're aiming to save $1 million by age 50, breaking it down annually, monthly, or even daily can transform a daunting goal into digestible pieces. Let's say you're 30 now. That gives you 20 years. You'd need to save about $50,000 a year, which breaks down to roughly $4,167 a month. Still a big number, right? But what if you look at it daily? That's about $137 a day. Suddenly, it seems a bit more achievable, especially if you're pulling in a doctor's salary.

Now, let's sprinkle in some stats to spice things up. Did you know that people who set specific saving goals can save up to 2x more as compared to those who don't? It's true. And here's another kicker: starting small actually makes you more likely to stick with it. It's the principle behind why apps like Duolingo or Fitness Challenges start you off with just 5 or

10 minutes a day. It's not just about making progress; it's about building the habit.

So, how do you start? First, automate your savings. Set up your accounts so a little bit gets tucked away into your savings or investment accounts with every paycheck. Out of sight, out of mind, but boy, does it add up.

Second, celebrate the small wins. Saved enough for one month of college for your kid? That's huge! Treat yourself to a little victory dance or a nice cup of coffee. These little rewards can boost your motivation and keep you on track.

Lastly, keep the big picture in perspective. Each small step you take is a piece of the puzzle in achieving your dream. It's not just about the $137 you save today; it's about the freedom, security, and peace of mind you're building for the Future You.

So, let's lace up those sneakers, take that first small step, and start the journey toward your big dreams. Remember, every big achievement was once just a dream coupled with a series of small, consistent actions. You've got this!

Know Your Why

Your goals need soul. Why do you want that million bucks? Is it the freedom to travel, the security of retirement without penny-pinching, or maybe the joy of helping your kids through college debt-free? Nearly 70% of people say they want to retire by 65, but only a fraction have a clear vision for their retirement.

"Your 'why' is your fuel. It transforms every saved dollar into a step toward your dreams—whether it's that beach house, family vacations, or simply peace of mind. Remember, you're not just stashing cash; you're actively building the life you crave. Let this purpose guide your budgeting and investing, making each decision a meaningful pursuit of your goals."

Imagine you're at a crossroads every payday: one path leads to immediate gratification—let's call it the "Instant Joy Lane". It's tempting, right? On the other side, there's a slightly less glamorous path, "Future Bliss Boulevard." Here's where your 'why' comes into play. It's the beacon that guides you down Future Bliss Boulevard, even when Instant Joy Lane is flashing neon lights at you.

Let's get real for a second. A study showed that people with a strong sense of purpose save more, invest wisely, and are less likely to splurge on impulsive buys. Why? Because every financial decision is weighed against the bigger picture. Will buying this shiny new gadget bring you closer to your dream home, or is it just a detour on your financial roadmap?

Now, think about what makes you tick. Is it the freedom to explore the world without the shackles of a 9-to-5 job? Or the ability to provide the best education to your kids? Maybe it's the security of knowing you won't have to rely on anyone in your golden years. Your 'why' is as unique as your fingerprint, and it's what makes your financial journey personal and powerful.

But here's a pro tip: write it down. Yep, scribble your 'why' on a sticky note, a journal, or even a digital note on your phone. A Harvard Business Study found that writing down your goals and dreams significantly increases your chances of achieving them. It's like making a pact with yourself, a constant reminder of what you're working so hard for.

In those moments of temptation, when Instant Joy Lane is beckoning, pull out your 'why.' Let it be the voice that says, "Hey, remember what we're here for?" It's about aligning your daily choices with your deepest aspirations, turning each financial decision into a stepping stone toward your dreams.

So, take a moment, reflect on your 'why,' and let it be the compass that navigates your financial decisions. Because when you know your 'why,' the 'how' becomes easier, and the journey? Well, it becomes an adventure.

Track, Tweak, Triumph

Here's the kicker: only 30% of people have a long-term financial plan with investment and savings goals. But guess what? Those are the folks who end up nailing their financial targets. The secret sauce? They keep tabs on their progress and aren't afraid to adjust their sails when the wind changes.

Set up regular check-ins with your financial goals. Maybe it's a monthly coffee date with your budget or a quarterly review with your wealth strategist. Spotted a snag? Tweak your plan. Found a windfall? Maybe you can speed up your timeline. The path to your goals isn't a straight line; it's a road with turns, hills, and the occasional speed bump. But with your eye on the prize and the willingness to adapt, you're set for the win.

It's all about making your financial journey as smooth as possible, with a healthy dose of realism and flexibility. Here's how you can keep your financial goals on track, tweak them when necessary, and ultimately triumph:

- **Follow the Power of Budgeting:** Think of your budget as your roadmap. Without it, you're just wandering. A shocking 65% of Americans don't know how much they spent last month. Keeping a budget helps you track where your money's going, and more importantly, it shows you where you can cut back or reallocate funds to fuel your goals. It's not about penny-pinching; it's about making your money work smarter.

- **Celebrate Small Wins:** Every journey is made up of steps, and every step towards your goal deserves a high five. Did you manage to save an extra $100 this month? That's a win! Small victories keep you motivated and make the process enjoyable. Remember, it's a marathon, not a sprint. Celebrating these milestones can boost your morale and keep you focused on the end game.

- **Stay Flexible with Your Strategies:** Life throws curveballs, and your financial plan should be ready to catch them. An unexpected medical bill, a sudden job change, or even a market downturn can throw a wrench in your plans. That's okay! Nearly 40% of people have to adjust their financial plans due to unforeseen circumstances. The key is to adapt your strategies, not abandon your goals. Maybe you can extend your timeline or find alternative income sources. Flexibility is your friend.

- **Leverage Technology:** There's an app for everything, including your finances. From budget trackers to investment apps, technology can simplify the tracking process. About 64% of smartphone users have at least one financial app. These tools offer real-time insights into your financial health, help you monitor investments, and even provide alerts for bill payments or budget caps. Let technology be your financial sidekick, keeping you informed and engaged.

- **Seek Professional Guidance:** Sometimes, a fresh pair of eyes can offer new perspectives. Whether it's a wealth strategist, a savvy friend, or an online community, getting external input can be invaluable. They can help you identify blind spots in your plan, suggest adjustments, and even introduce you to strategies you hadn't considered. The goal is to make informed decisions that align with your financial vision.

In the dance of finance, tracking your progress, tweaking your strategies, and celebrating your triumphs are the steps to success. By staying engaged, adaptable, and informed, you're not just chasing your goals; you're paving a path toward them. Keep your eyes on the prize, and let's turn those financial dreams into reality, one smart move at a time.

Hey, just a reminder, if you didn't download the financial guide, which has places for you to, to execute on all these and put something on paper, click here.

1.3 Cultivating Financial Confidence

Navigating the world of finance can feel like learning a new language, especially for us docs who've spent years mastering the art of medicine, not money. But guess what? Financial confidence isn't some exclusive club. It's a skill, and like any skill, it's something you can totally get the hang of. How about we simplify this step-by-step?

Starting Small: Baby Steps to Big Wins

Think about the first time you held a scalpel. Daunting, right? But with practice, it became second nature. Finance is no different. Start with the basics: budgeting, saving, and understanding debt. Did you know that a simple budget can help you save 10-20% more each month? That's like giving yourself a raise without even asking the boss. And savings? Let's not even talk about the peace of mind that comes from having a rainy day fund. Start small, celebrate those wins, and watch your confidence soar.

Let's dive a bit deeper into how these initial steps can set you on a path to financial confidence and success. Every giant leap starts with a small step. Here are some actionable strategies to get you moving:

- **Automate Your Savings:** One of the simplest yet most effective strategies is to automate your savings. Think of it as a "set it and forget it" approach. By setting up automatic transfers to your savings account, you're paying yourself first, putting your financial growth on autopilot. And the best part? You won't miss what you don't see. Before you know it, you'll have a nice cushion that can give you peace of mind or serve as capital for future investments.

- **Crush That Debt with the Snowball** Method: Start with your smallest debt, and once it's paid off, roll the amount you were paying on it into the next smallest debt. It's like a snowball rolling down a hill, gathering size and momentum. This method not only helps you reduce your debt but also provides psychological wins that boost your confidence. According to a study by the Harvard Business Review, the snowball method is surprisingly effective, not just in theory but in practice.

- **Track Your Spending:** You can't manage what you don't measure. By keeping an eye on where your money is going each month, you can identify and cut back on unnecessary expenses. Simple tools like budgeting apps or spreadsheets can be incredibly powerful. Did you know that regular budget tracking can help uncover hidden leaks in your finances that could be costing you up to 20% of your monthly income? That's like finding free money that you can redirect towards your financial goals.

- **Start Investing, Even If It's Just a Little:** Thanks to modern technology, you don't need thousands of dollars to start investing. Apps and platforms now allow you to invest with as little as $5. And while that might not sound like much, remember the power of compound interest. Over time, even small amounts can grow significantly. For instance, if you invest just $50 a month with an average return of 7% (the historical average of the stock market), you could have over $23,000 in 20 years. Imagine what you could do if you increased that amount over time!

- **Educate Yourself Financially:** Dedicate a small portion of your week to learning about personal finance and investing. This doesn't mean you need to enroll in a finance degree. There are countless free resources online, from articles and ebooks to webinars and YouTube channels, all geared towards beginners. Knowledge is not just power; it's profit. A survey by the National Financial Educators Council found that individuals who invested time in financial education saved an average of $1,200 in a year just by making more informed financial decisions.

By focusing on these small, manageable steps, you're not just working towards financial security; you're building a foundation of financial confidence that will empower you to make smarter, bolder financial decisions in the future. The journey of a thousand miles begins with just a single step. So, take that step today, and let's start walking towards your financial freedom together!

Knowledge is Power: Learning to Love the Lingo

Alright, let's tackle the elephant in the room: investment jargon. Stocks, bonds, mutual funds... it can all seem like gibberish. But here's a secret: you don't need to be a Wall Street whiz to make smart investment choices. Dive into some finance blogs, grab a few beginner-friendly books, or even join a local investment club. The more you learn, the less intimidating it all becomes. Remember, even Warren Buffett started somewhere, and he's been quoted saying that you don't need to be a genius to invest wisely. You just need to learn the ropes.

You see, the finance world loves its acronyms and fancy terms—ETFs, ROIs, dividends, you name it. But here's a little secret: once you peel back the jargon, the concepts are often straightforward. It's like when you first learned medical terms. Remember how "subcutaneous" sounded so complex, only to find out it just meant "under the skin"? Finance is similar. For instance, "ETFs" are just baskets of stocks you can buy and sell, kind of like a pre-made smoothie mix; you get a variety of fruits without having to buy each one separately.

Now, let's talk about why this matters. Studies suggest that a lack of financial literacy can cost individuals an average of $10,200 a year in poor financial decisions. That's a mini-vacation you're missing out on! But here's the uplifting part: dedicating just a few hours a week to learning about finance can significantly boost your financial literacy. Podcasts during your commute, audiobooks on your jog, or even YouTube tutorials while you unwind can all be easy, low-effort ways to start absorbing the lingo.

And let's not forget about the power of community. Joining online forums or local investment clubs can be incredibly enriching. It's like being part of a study group back in med school; everyone's sharing notes, discussing complex topics, and suddenly, things start clicking. Plus, it's reported that individuals who discuss financial matters with peers are 23% more likely to feel confident in their financial decisions. That's a pretty solid boost in confidence for just talking shop with fellow finance learners!

So, follow the lingo, get curious, and remember that every new term you learn is a tool in your financial toolkit. Before you know it, you'll be slinging finance terms with ease, making informed decisions, and maybe even helping your colleagues demystify their own financial puzzles. Knowledge truly is power, especially when it comes to securing your financial future.

Following Mistakes: The Stepping Stones to Success

Here's a truth bomb: you're going to make mistakes. And that's okay! Every misstep is a chance to learn. You might invest in a stock that tanks or buy into a trend too late. It happens to the best of us. In fact, a study showed that most investors make a significant mistake in their first year. But guess what? They learn, adapt, and come back stronger. The key is to not let the fear of failure hold you back. Consider the bumps in the road as part of your journey to financial savvy.

Here's the thing: Remember when you first learned to ride a bike? Chances are, you didn't just hop on and take off without a single wobble or fall. In much the same way, messing up with your money is pretty much expected when you're just starting out. Mistakes are a part of the learning process, and they can provide valuable lessons that help you manage your finances more effectively in the long run."

Learning on the Go

So, you made a not-so-great investment choice, or perhaps you waited too long to sell something. It happens. The key is to not beat yourself up about it. Instead, ask yourself, "What can I learn from this?" It's like watching a replay of a game to spot where things went sideways. This isn't just about avoiding the same mistake twice; it's about getting sharper and smarter for the next round.

Building Your Safety Net

Now, about keeping those risks in check—think of it as wearing knee pads and a helmet when you're learning to skate. You might still take a tumble, but it won't hurt as much. In money terms, this means not throwing all your cash into one thing. Spread it out a bit. That way, if one thing doesn't pan out, it's not game over. And hey, setting up some "rules" for yourself, like a limit on how much you're okay with losing, can help keep things from getting too dicey.

Celebrate Each Step Forward

Remember, each small victory is a sign of progress. Whether it's mastering your budget for the first time or earning a profit that allows for a small celebration, each success is important. Celebrating these achievements reinforces positive habits and keeps you motivated on your financial journey. Consider these moments as milestones in your path to becoming financially savvy.

Remember, everyone who's good at something was once a beginner, making plenty of mistakes along the way. The trick is to keep at it, learn from the missteps, and not let them scare you off. Keep your head up, learn as you go, and pretty soon, you'll be amazed at how far you've come.

Next Up: Making Your Money Work

Alright, so we've talked about getting comfortable with the ups and downs. Now, what's next? As we wrap up our deep dive into cultivating financial confidence, remember: it's all about starting small, following the learning curve, and seeing every mistake as a step forward, not back. You're building a solid foundation, one brick at a time, transforming that initial trepidation into a well-earned sense of empowerment.

But our journey doesn't end here. Oh no, we're just getting warmed up! As we pivot from the basics of financial confidence, we're about to embark on an even more exhilarating adventure: shaping your wealth mindset.

As we dissect the daunting mountain of med school debt and strategize on goal setting, it's pivotal to highlight an often-overlooked avenue that could revolutionize your financial journey: alternative investments. The stats speak volumes; between 1986 and 2022, private equity outshone the S&P 500 by a significant margin, delivering a 14.28% return compared to 9.2%. That's not just a win; it's a game-changer, offering a 50% greater return. Moreover, private credit has emerged as a powerhouse, yielding two to three times the income of traditional bonds. These figures aren't mere numbers; they're a testament to the untapped potential that lies beyond conventional investment paths, promising a more robust financial pulse for those ready to explore.

Ready to take control of your financial future? Join us today and become part of a community dedicated to helping you achieve financial freedom and live the life you deserve. Once you experience success, share your wins with the group and inspire others on their journey!

Scan the QR code to join our facebook group and start your journey to financial empowerment!

Case Study

Case Study 1: Dr. Emily's Budgeting Breakthrough

Meet Dr. Emily, a cardiologist who always felt that her finances were running her, not the other way around. With student loans looming large and her savings looking slim, she decided it was time for a change. Emily started with something simple: tracking her spending. She used a basic budgeting app and was shocked to discover that small, everyday expenses were adding up to a huge chunk of her monthly income.

By trimming these expenses and setting a budget, Emily managed to increase her savings rate by 15% in just six months. This small step gave her the confidence boost she needed to tackle bigger financial goals, proving that a little awareness can lead to big changes.

Case Study 2: Dr. Jordan's Investment Journey

Next up is Dr. Jordan, an orthopedic surgeon who admitted to knowing more about bones than about bonds. The investing world felt intimidating, filled with jargon he didn't understand. But Jordan didn't let that stop him. He started attending local finance workshops and getting in touch with people that could help.

Six months in, Jordan made his first investment partnering with a group of other doctors and a small apartment complex in Texas, a simple choice that matched his risk tolerance and long-term goals. A year later, Jordan's portfolio had grown by 14%, a modest but thrilling start to his investment journey. Jordan's story is a testament to the power of starting small and the value of community in demystifying the investment process.

Case Study 3: Dr. Brett Learning Curve

Lastly, let's talk about Dr. Brett, a dedicated family physician who experienced a significant financial setback when an investment didn't pan out as expected. Rather than letting this discourage him, Dr. Brett saw it as a learning opportunity. He took a step back to analyze what went wrong and realized he'd jumped in without fully understanding the investment or partnering with somebody who understood.

Determined to turn the situation around, Dr. Brett dedicated time each week to financial education, reading books, attending seminars, and listening to podcasts. This commitment to learning transformed his approach to investing, making him more cautious and informed. Within a couple of years, not only had he recovered his lost investment, but he'd also built a diverse portfolio that was steadily growing.

Chapter 2: The Wealth Mindset

Welcome to Chapter 2, we're going on a little adventure into the land of the Wealth Mindset. It's like upgrading your mental software to the latest, greatest version, specifically designed for wealth-building. We're going to tackle some pretty cool stuff that could totally change the game for you.

First up, we're going to talk about breaking free from traditional investment strategies that have been failing doctors for decades. We are going to explore. I'm mixing it up with a diversified portfolio that will not only decrease your risk but also increase your return compared to traditional investments such as the S&P index. According to Ray Dalio's principles, diversifying your portfolio into assets that are not correlated with each other can reduce your risk by up to 80%. This means that for every unit of risk you take, you could potentially get five times the return. Yep, It's a thing.

Then, we're going to sneak up on that sneaky little bugger called lifestyle creep. It's when your spending starts to sneakily inch up as your paycheck grows, leaving you wondering where all your money went at the end of the month. We'll chat about some ninja moves to keep your spending in check without missing out on the joys of life.

And finally, we're going to get cozy with risk and reward. It's like learning to love a bit of spice in your food. A little can make all the difference, but you gotta find the right balance. We'll dive into how taking calculated risks can be the secret sauce to juicing up your returns, without giving you financial indigestion.

So, are you ready to shake things up and give your wealth-building strategy a major upgrade? Let's do this!

2.1 Overcoming Traditional Constraints

Hey! Want to know how I reverse-engineered success? Scan this QR code to watch my video where I share my journey and insights on achieving financial freedom. In this video, you'll learn practical tips and strategies that have helped me and many others take control of our financial futures. Don't miss out on this valuable content!

Let's talk about the usual path that has failed doctors', "traditional investments". It's like sticking to the kiddie pool when there's a whole ocean out there. Sure. It's comfortable to be a lemming and follow what the crowd is doing, but the crowd doesn't retire early and they take unnecessary risks unknowingly. Some stocks, bonds, maybe some real estate. Traditional investments like mutual fund portfolios and a handful of bonds may be adequate, but why not consider diversifying with more alternative investments? This strategy is where the big players—like the endowments of Harvard, Yale, and Stanford—invest up to 80 percent of their portfolios, and with good reason. They have access to the best investment advice money can buy.

"When we discuss the idea of not relying solely on safe investments, consider it like this: If you only put your money in places that feel super safe, like savings accounts or bonds, Think of it as limiting yourself to just one ice cream flavor forever. Sure, it's good, but there are so many other flavors out there! Mixing things up a bit with different kinds of investments can make your money work harder for you.

If you're worried about making a bad choice, that's totally normal. But here's a cool thing about spreading your investments around: if one doesn't do so great, you've got others that can still do well. It's like having a bunch of different tools in your toolbox. If one tool doesn't fit, you've got others that might do the job better.

And here's something else to think about: if your money isn't growing enough, it might not keep up with the prices going up over time, which is something called inflation. Inflation happens because the value of the dollar goes down as the government keeps printing more dollars. It's like if you're walking on a moving sidewalk at the airport. If you stand still, you'll move a bit because of the sidewalk, but if you walk a little, you'll go much faster. You want your money to be walking, not just standing!

So, how do you start trying out these different investment "flavors"? It's all about learning one bit at a time. You don't have to become an expert overnight. Your situation is unique, so what works for one person might not be the best for you. If all this sounds a bit much, it's okay to ask for help. A wealth strategist can help make a plan that fits just right for you.

In short, it's good to be careful with your money, but a little bit of variety in your investments can really help. Think about what feels right for you, learn bit by bit, and don't be afraid to ask for advice. Ready to give it a try?

- **Spread Your Investments:** Just as you wouldn't wear the same outfit for every occasion, you shouldn't put all your money into one type of investment. Diversifying your portfolio can help manage risk and enhance potential returns.

- **Learn About Alternatives and other investment options:** Stocks, real estate, and bonds are just the start. There's a whole world out there.

- **Check Inflation:** Your money needs to grow faster than prices rise, otherwise, it's like running on a treadmill – lots of effort, going nowhere.

- **Small Steps:** You don't have to dive in all at once. Start with small changes to your investment plan.

- **Mistakes Happen:** It's part of learning. The key is not to put all your money in one place, so a mistake doesn't trip you up completely.

- **Advice Can Help:** Talking to a wealth strategist can give you personalized tips that fit just right for your situation.

- **Keep Learning:** The more you know, the better choices you'll make. And today, online resources have made investing easier than ever

- **Stay Patient:** Good investing isn't about getting rich quickly. It's about steady growth over time.

- **Review and Adjust:** Your needs will change as you get closer to retirement. Keep an eye on your investments and tweak them as needed.

- **Enjoy the Journey:** Remember, investing is a means to an end – living the life you want. Keep your goals in sight and adjust your approach as you go.

2.2 Escaping Lifestyle Creep

Now, onto lifestyle creep. It's sneaky. One day you're living on ramen and the next, you're pondering which Tesla model suits your vibe. Here's the kicker: as your paycheck grows, so does the temptation to splurge. Happens to the best of us. But remember, every dollar spent on today's luxuries is a dollar not invested in your future freedom. It's like eating the seeds meant for planting. It might satisfy you now, but it leaves you with nothing for next season's harvest. So, how about we outsmart this creep? Start by automating your savings. Before you know it, you'll have a hefty nest egg growing, all while enjoying the finer things in life, sensibly.

Budgeting Like a Boss

First up, let's get real about budgeting. I know, I know, the word "budget" might sound like a party pooper, but hear me out. It's actually your secret weapon against lifestyle creep. Think of it as your financial GPS, helping you navigate where your money's going each month. Did you know that a simple budget can help you save upwards of 20% more each year? That's right. By tracking your spending, you're less likely to splurge on those impulse buys and more likely to stash that cash for your future self. So, grab a pen, an app, or even a napkin, and start plotting your financial roadmap.

...And if you haven't downloaded our Financial Roadmap you can get it here:

let's break down some key strategies:

- **Track Every Penny:** It might sound tedious, but knowing where every dollar goes is eye-opening. A survey found that folks who track their spending can cut their expenses by 15% just by being aware of where their money is slipping through the cracks. So, start jotting down those daily lattes, online subscriptions, and even those sneaky vending machine snacks. It's all about visibility and control.

- **Automate Your Savings:** This one's a game-changer. Set up your accounts so a chunk of your paycheck automatically dives into your savings or investment account before you even see it. Think of it as a magic trick where part of your money invisibly moves to where it can grow, out of the reach of impulse buys. Automation is like putting your savings on autopilot, ensuring you're consistently building that nest egg without the monthly willpower battle.

- **Give Every Dollar a Job:** This is about being intentional with your income. Instead of money just hanging around in your account, waiting to be spent, assign it a purpose. Whether it's for rent, groceries, savings, or even a little fun money, every dollar should have its mission. This approach not only helps prevent frivolous spending but also ensures you're allocating enough to your big-picture goals.

- **Follow the 50/30/20 Rule:** Here's a simple blueprint for where your money should go. Allocate about 50% of your take-home pay to necessities, 30% to wants, and stash away 20% for savings or paying off debt. It's a flexible framework that keeps you grounded, ensuring you're living within your means while still enjoying life and securing your future.

- **Regular Financial Check-ins:** Treat your budget like a living, breathing thing. It needs care and attention. Set aside time each month to review your spending, adjust for any changes in your financial landscape, and celebrate the wins, no matter how small. These check-ins keep you accountable and allow you to tweak your budget to better fit your evolving life and goals.

The Joy of Saying "No"

"Saying "no" isn't about missing out; it's about making sure you're winning on what really matters to you." -Amir Baluch, MD

Now, onto mastering the art of saying "no." It's tough, especially when you're surrounded by shiny new gadgets, exotic vacations, and that fancy new restaurant everyone's talking about. But here's the thing: every "no" to unnecessary spending is a resounding "yes" to your financial freedom. It's about prioritizing what really matters to you. Is it that new iPhone, or is it the freedom to work because you want to, not because you have to? Remember, it's not about depriving yourself but about making conscious choices. You'll be amazed at how empowering it feels to take control of your spending, one "no" at a time.

Let's keep it simple and real. Saying "no" is pretty much like having a superpower without needing a cape. It's all about making choices that really work for you, not just because everyone else is doing it or because that flashy ad said you should.

- **Cash Stays in Your Pocket:** Every "no" means more money hanging out in your bank account. Skip that fancy coffee once a week, and boom, you've got yourself an extra few hundred bucks at the end of the year.

- **Chill Mode:** Overspending is a one-way ticket to Stressville. Keep it chill by keeping your spending in check. Less money worries = more peace of mind.

- **Goals on Track:** Every time you pass on something you don't need, you're one step closer to the big stuff, like that dream vacation or even retiring early. Small wins add up.

- **Enjoying What You've Got:** It's easy to forget about all the cool stuff you already have when you're always looking for the next best thing. Saying "no" helps you remember and appreciate what's right in front of you.

- **You're the Boss:** Remember, you're in charge of your money, not the other way around. Saying "no" means you're making the calls, not those flashy ads or the latest trends.

So, next time you're about to say "yes" to something you're not sure about, just remember how good it feels to be in control.

Investing in Experiences, Not Things

Lastly, let's shift our focus from accumulating things to creating memorable experiences. Studies have shown that people who spend money on experiences, like a family vacation or learning a new skill, report higher levels of happiness and satisfaction than those who splurge on material goods. Why? because the joy from experiences tends to grow over time as you reminisce and share stories, unlike the fleeting thrill of a new purchase that quickly fades. So, next time you're about to click "buy" on that latest gadget, pause and ask yourself: could this money bring me more joy elsewhere? Maybe it's that scuba diving course you've always wanted to take or a weekend getaway with loved ones. Investing in experiences not only enriches your life but also helps keep lifestyle creep at bay, ensuring your financial goals remain within reach.

Picking up from "Investing in Experiences, Not Things," it's all about flipping the script on what truly adds value to our lives. Imagine looking back years from now; it is the adventures and moments that'll shine the brightest in your memory, not the stuff that filled your space. It's like choosing between a shiny, new watch and a weekend exploring a new city. Fast forward a few years, and it's the laughter, the sights, the mishaps, and the stories from that trip that will still warm your heart, long after the watch has lost its luster. This isn't just feel-good advice; it's backed by research showing that experiences contribute to our happiness much more than material goods ever could. So, let's make a conscious effort to invest in life's real treasures – the moments that bring us joy, growth, and connection.

Here are five ways to start shifting towards more experiential living:

- **Prioritize 'Doing' Over 'Having':** Next time you're about to make a significant purchase, pause and consider if you could use that money for an experience instead. Could that new home theater system budget take your family on a camping trip, creating memories to last a lifetime?

- **Experience Over Expensive:** Remember, experiences don't have to break the bank to be meaningful. A picnic in the park with friends can be just as enriching as an expensive concert. It's the quality of the experience, not the price tag, that counts.

- **Learn Something New:** Investing in learning new skills or hobbies not only enriches your life but also expands your horizons and connects you with like-minded individuals. Whether it's cooking classes, photography, or sailing, the joy and satisfaction from mastering a new skill can far outweigh the pleasure of a new purchase.

- **Give Experiences as Gifts:** Next time you're gift shopping, think about gifting an experience, like concert tickets, a cooking class, or a day at the spa. It's a wonderful way to show you care, encouraging others to create beautiful memories.

- **Document and Share Your Experiences:** Make it a point to capture the moments, either through photos, journaling, or even social media shares. Not only does it help you relive those experiences, but it also inspires others to prioritize joy and connection in their own lives.

By consciously choosing experiences over things, we're not just avoiding lifestyle creep; we're actively crafting a life that's rich in stories, learning and connections. It's these moments that become the fabric of our lives, bringing us genuine happiness and getting us closer to a fulfilling early retirement.

2.3 Follow Risk and Reward Asymmetric Returns

Alright, let's dive into the risk and reward tango. It's like spicy food; a little bit can add a whole lot of flavor, but too much? Hello, GERD. Investing's the same. Avoiding risk might feel cozy, but it's like leaving your car in neutral – you're not going anywhere fast. Here's something to chew on: historically, the stock market has given an average annual return of around 7-10% before inflation. Not too shabby, right? But with higher returns comes higher risk. The key? Finding your sweet spot. It's about balancing high-reward investments with safer bets to keep your financial goals on track without losing sleep. Think of it as having the right mix of spices in your investment recipe.

Let's dive deeper into making risk your ally in the quest for financial freedom.

Finding Your Risk Comfort Zone

First up, let's chat about comfort zones. You know, that cozy spot where everything feels safe and sound. But here's the deal: too comfy, and growth takes a backseat. It's like sticking to the bunny slopes when you could be shredding down the mountain. The trick is to nudge your boundaries just enough to up the ante without causing a panic. Think about it - if you can handle a bit of market turbulence without losing sleep, you might be ready to dial up the risk a tad. But if the mere thought makes your stomach churn, it's cool to take it slow. Remember, it's not about keeping up with the Joneses; it's about what works for you.

When we talk about getting comfy with risk, it's like adjusting the temperature in your shower. Too cold, and it's no fun; too hot, and well, ouch. It's all about finding that just right setting. So, how can you do that with your investments? First off, take a good look at where you're at. Are you the kind of person who checks your investment app every hour, or do you forget about it for months? If you're the first type, you might want to ease up a bit on the risk to keep your sanity. But if you're more laid-back, you could most likely handle a bit more action in your portfolio.

Think about your goals. If you're saving up for something big in the near future, like a dream vacation or a new car, you might want to play it safer. But if you're looking at the long haul, like retirement, you've got time on your side. Here's a fun fact: over the last 100 years, the stock market has returned about 10% a year on average. But remember, that's a roller coaster ride with plenty of ups and downs along the way.

Here's a few pointers to keep in mind as you figure out your comfort zone:

- **Baby Steps:** Start with a mix that feels okay and tweak it as you go. There's no rush.
- **Learn as You Go:** The more you know, the less scary it feels. A little bit of homework can go a long way.
- **Keep it Cool:** If checking your investments is making you anxious, you might need to dial back the risk.
- **What's the Plan?:** Keep your eyes on the prize. Knowing what you're investing for can help you stick to your plan.
- **Check-In, But Not Too Often:** Give your investments some breathing room. Constantly watching the market is like watching paint dry — not very exciting and pretty pointless.

In the end, It's crucial to make the right decisions for your portfolio, even if they make you uncomfortable.. No need to be a hero and dive into the deep end right away. Take your time, find your groove, and remember, it's all about the journey, not just the destination.

Balancing Act: Diversification and Allocation

Now, let's talk about the balancing act. Imagine you're at a buffet. You wouldn't pile your plate with just one dish, right? Investing is similar; you've got to mix it up because diversification is your best pal here. By spreading your investments across different asset classes, you're not putting all your eggs in one basket. And here's where it gets spicy: allocation. It's all about the mix. Maybe you're 50% private equity, 30% private credit, and 20% other stuff like real estate or gold. But as you edge closer to retirement, you might want to shift that mix to play it a bit safer. It's like adjusting your sail as the wind changes. Keep it dynamic, keep it balanced.

It's crucial to get this mix just right for your financial health. Think of diversification as your investment diet. Just like you need fruits, veggies, proteins, and carbs for a balanced diet, your portfolio needs a variety of assets to stay healthy. Private or public stocks, bonds, real estate, and maybe some precious metals or cryptocurrencies can all play a part. The key is not to overload on any one thing. Sure, stocks might give you a great run some years, but they can also take a nosedive. That's where bonds or real estate can help steady the ship, keeping your portfolio afloat when the stock market gets choppy.

Allocation takes this concept a step further. It's not just about having a bit of everything; it's about having the right amounts of each, tailored to your personal financial goals and how much time you have to reach them. As you move closer to retirement, you might want to shift more into asset classes that spin off monthly or quarterly cash flow so you can peel back time from work. You start off pedaling hard for long-term growth, but as you near your destination, you might shift to an easier gear with steady payouts to ensure a smooth arrival.

The problem is that today most traditional diversification strategies tend to involve adding more and more positively correlated investments! Some investors, knowingly or not, seem to have given up on finding uncorrelated investments to help manage big swings. One frightening headline recently came across my newsfeed: Older Americans, those in retirement or near to it, are forgoing bonds for protection and betting most or all of their future solely on stocks.

Here are five bullet points to keep in mind:

- **Diversify Across Sectors and Geographies:** Don't just stick to one industry or country. Spread your investments across different sectors and global markets to reduce risk.

- **Regularly Rebalance Your Portfolio:** As some investments grow, they can become too large a part of your portfolio. Regular rebalancing helps maintain your desired risk level.

- **Consider Your Time Horizon:** The closer you are to needing your money (like retirement), the more conservative your allocation should be. Also, you need to add cash flows. You're getting close to retirement, be a little bit conservative and focus more on cash flows.

- **Stay Informed but Don't Overreact:** Keep up with financial news and trends, but avoid knee-jerk reactions to short-term market fluctuations. Stick to your long-term strategy.

By keeping these principles in mind, you can create a portfolio that's not just diversified, but also perfectly aligned with your financial journey and goals. It's about making your money work for you, across all seasons of your life.

Follow the Long Game

Finally, let's talk about the long game. Investing is not a sprint; it's a marathon. And in this marathon, time is your secret weapon. Thanks to the magic of compounding, even small investments can balloon into a hefty sum over the years. The key is to stay the course, keep your eyes on the prize, and not bail at the first sign of trouble.

So, there you have it: finding your comfort zone, mixing it up with diversification, and playing the long game. It's about making informed choices, staying patient, and sometimes taking that leap. Let's make your financial journey an adventure worth telling!

Patience isn't just a virtue; it's a strategy. Think of it like planting a tree— you water it regularly and wait for it to grow. The same goes for your investments. Those little seeds you're sowing now, with regular contributions and a steady hand, will eventually flourish.

- Find your comfort zone.
- Diversify your portfolio.
- Play the long game.
- Make informed choices.
- Stay patient.
- Take calculated risks.

- Contribute regularly.
- Maintain a steady hand.

- **Consistency is key:** Regular contributions, even small ones, can significantly impact due to compound interest.

- **Market timing is a myth:** Trying to guess the market's highs and lows is less effective as compared to consistent, long-term investment. If anything, it's generally more about time in the market vs timing the market.

- **Rebalancing matters:** Periodically adjusting your portfolio to maintain your desired risk level keeps you on track.

- **Stay informed, not reactive:** Keep an eye on the market trends but avoid reactions to short-term volatility.

- **Trust in the process:** The market has historically trended upwards over long periods, so trust in the resilience and growth potential of your investments.

As you navigate your financial journey, remember that the most successful investors aren't necessarily the ones making the flashiest moves. They're the ones with a plan they stick to, through thick and thin, focused on their long-term goals. It's this steadfast approach that turns today's investments into tomorrow's treasures.

Chapter 3: The Alchemy of Money

Hey there, fellow healers of humanity! It's Dr. Amir Baluch here, your guide on this thrilling expedition to financial freedom. Let's dive into the magic realm where your money doesn't just sit there; it grows, multiplies, and works harder than a caffeine-fueled med student on a 36-hour shift. Welcome to "The Alchemy of Money."

3.1 Maximizing Investment Opportunities

First off, let's chat about maxing out those investment opportunities. Picture your retirement accounts like a buffet at a medical conference. You wouldn't just stick to the salad bar, right? Dive into the whole spread! 401(k)s, IRAs, and maybe even a Roth, if you're feeling adventurous. Here's a juicy nugget: folks who max out their retirement contributions can end up with a stash 25% larger than the average bear. Why leave free money on the table, especially when it comes with a side of tax breaks?

Diving deeper into "Maximizing Investment Opportunities," let's unwrap this like it's the best gift under the financial freedom tree:

Variety is the Spice of Investing: Here's why:

- Spreading your investments across alternative variations such as private equity, real estate, fixed-income products, private credit, notes, oil, and gas can cushion you against market hiccups. Think of it like having both a raincoat and sunscreen in your bag – ready for any weather.

- Investing in international markets opens up a world of opportunities. Did you know that emerging markets have shown growth rates that often outpace developed ones? It's like discovering a hidden gem in an old textbook.

- Sector-specific funds allow you to capitalize on booming industries. Healthcare advancements such as biotech funds might just be your golden goose.

- Life insurance policies with investment options, like variable or universal life, offer a unique way to tap into the stock market. If your net worth is above $5M you may want to consider premium finance of life insurance, where banks will loan you money to put into a cash value policy that compounds over time.

- Remember, the aim is to build a portfolio that aligns with your risk tolerance and retirement goals, kind of like choosing the right specialty that suits your passion and lifestyle.

Timing is Everything – But Not in the Way You Think: *Timing the market is like trying to predict the weather based on yesterday's forecast – often wrong and always frustrating.*

Instead, consider these points:

"It's more about time in the market than timing the market"

- Consistent investment over time, through the highs and lows, smooths out the market's ups and downs. It's the financial equivalent of steady hands in surgery.

- Reinvesting dividends and profits can supercharge your portfolio's growth, turning small gains into a snowballing wealth avalanche over time.

- Long-term investing reduces the impact of short-term volatility, ensuring that temporary market dips don't derail your retirement plans. It's about keeping your eye on the horizon, not the waves at your feet.

- Patience pays off. Studies have shown that long-term investors typically see more substantial returns than those who jump in and out of the market. Imagine planting a tree; you don't dig it up every few weeks to check on the roots.

Knowledge is Power – Stay Informed and Engaged: Keeping abreast of financial news and trends can empower you to make informed decisions.

Here's how to stay on top of your investment game:

- Regularly review your investment portfolio to ensure it aligns with your evolving financial goals and life changes. It's akin to a regular health check-up.

- Educate yourself on tax-advantaged accounts and strategies to maximize post-tax returns. Knowing the ins and outs of an HSA, for instance, can save you a bundle in taxes.

- Consider working with a wealth and tax strategist to navigate complex investment landscapes, much like consulting a specialist for a challenging case.

- Stay updated on economic indicators and market trends, but avoid knee-jerk reactions to news. It's about using data to inform decisions, not dictate them.

- Follow continuous learning. The world of finance is always evolving, and staying informed is key to adapting and thriving. Whether through podcasts, books, or webinars, keep feeding your financial knowledge.

By focusing on these aspects, you're not just investing money; you're investing in a future where financial freedom and early retirement aren't just possible—they're within reach. Remember, the journey to wealth is a marathon, not a sprint. Pace yourself, stay informed, and watch as your investment efforts compound into a legacy of prosperity.

It's clear that diving into alternative investments like private equity, real estate, and private credit isn't just a trend—it's a smart move for savvy investors.

"An investment in knowledge pays the best interest."
– Benjamin Franklin

Here's a nugget to ponder: back in 2006, private equity was a smaller pool with about $1 trillion managed by pros. Fast forward, and it's ballooned to over $6 trillion. Even more jaw-dropping is the prediction that we're heading towards a whopping $14 trillion in the next few years in private equity alone.

Now, let's talk about where the big players put their money. Imagine having over $30 million to invest. Sounds like a dream, right? Well, those with that kind of cash, stash nearly 46-80% of it in alternative investments, leaving traditional as a minority portion of their portfolio. And guess where most of that alternative investment cash goes? A whopping 52% dives straight into private equity, with the rest split between real estate and hedge funds.

But here's the kicker: private equity hasn't just been a good choice; it's been a stellar one. Over the last 35 years, private equity has consistently outperformed public markets. We're talking about an impressive average annual return of 17.5% for private equity over the past decade, compared to 10.5% for the S&P 500. These figures highlight the potential for significantly higher returns in private equity investments, backed by data from leading financial research firms such as Cambridge Associates and Preqin. That might not seem like a huge difference at first glance, but over time, it's massive. Picture this: a $1 million investment in the S&P 500 would have grown to over $26 million by 2022. Impressive, right? But that same million in private equity? It would have skyrocketed to nearly $140 million.

So, what's the takeaway here? It's not just about throwing your money into the investment ring and hoping for the best. It's about making informed, strategic choices that align with your financial goals and risk tolerance. It's about seeing beyond the conventional and embracing the opportunities that alternative investments offer.

As we close this chapter, remember: investing is a journey, not a sprint. It's about growth, learning, and adapting. And with the insights we've shared, you're better equipped to navigate the path to financial prosperity.

Ready to take the leap into smarter investing? Let's make those numbers work for you. Here's to building a future where your financial dreams aren't just dreams—they're your reality.

3.2 Strategic Debt Management

Now, let's switch gears to debt. That big, scary D-word that haunts us like the ghost of bad decisions past. But here's the kicker – not all debt is created equal. Got student loans at 2% interest? Maybe chill on paying those off so quickly... But if you've got credit card debt creeping up at 20%, it's time to go full ninja on it. It's all about balance. Like deciding between ordering another round of blood tests or just asking your patient how they're feeling. Sometimes, the best move is the simplest one.

Got it, let's keep it real and chat more like we're swapping stories over a cup of coffee.

So, diving back into this whole debt juggling act, think of it like you're triaging in the ER. You've got some debts screaming at you like a patient with a paper cut thinking it's the end of the world, while others are more like that chill dude with a broken arm, patiently waiting his turn. Those high-interest debts, especially credit card ones? They're your paper cuts gone rogue. With interest rates soaring as high as 20% (crazy, right?), they can swell up faster than a bad allergic reaction if you don't slap a financial bandage on them ASAP.

Now, not all debts are out to get you. Your student loans or mortgage might feel like a heavyweight, but with interest rates often lounging around the 3% to 5% mark, they're more like that long-term patient who's in for the slow treatment plan. If you've got some extra dough, you might be tempted to throw it all at these debts but hold up. Imagine if you could invest that cash and maybe snag a 7% return. Suddenly, you're not just clearing debt; you're building a little treasure chest on the side. It's like choosing between a guaranteed small win or playing for a bigger prize with a bit of risk. Makes you think, huh?

And hey, let's not forget about that emergency fund – your financial safety net. Think of it as keeping a stash of those super-strong antibiotics for a rainy day. Life loves to throw curveballs, and without a little cushion (think 3-6 months of living expenses), you might find yourself reaching for the credit card and spiraling back into debt. It's all about striking that balance, keeping enough in the tank to handle the surprises without going back to square one.

To tackle your debt with numbers and a straightforward approach, here's a condensed guide:

1. List Each Debt: Write down what you owe, the interest rate, and the minimum payment. For example:

- Debt 1: $5,000 at 10% interest, $100 minimum payment.
- Debt 2: $2,000 at 15% interest, $40 minimum payment.

2. Calculate Monthly Interest: Use the formula:

Monthly Interest = (Interest Rate/12) X Debt

So for Debt 1, it's (10%/12) X $5,000 = $41.67.

3. Decide Extra Payment: Figure out how much more you can pay on top of minimum payments. Suppose it's $200.

4. Pick a Strategy (Snowball or Avalanche):

- **Snowball:** Pay minimums on all; put an extra $200 towards the smallest debt (Debt 2).
- **Avalanche:** Pay minimums on all; put an extra $200 towards the highest interest debt (Debt 2).

5. Update Balances Monthly: After payments, subtract what you've paid (including extra) from each debt, adding back the monthly interest. For Debt 2:

New Balance = $2,000 - ($40 + $200 - Monthly Interest)

6. Repeat: Keep going until all debts are paid. Redirect funds from cleared debts to the next target.

So there you have it, tackling debt with a bit of strategy, a bit of caution, and always keeping an eye on the prize. It's not just about clearing those numbers; it's about setting yourself up for a chill, worry-free financial vibe.

Let's keep this chat rolling and add a few more nuggets to our debt management strategy.

- First up, let's talk about snowballing. Ever made a snowball and rolled it down a hill? Starts small, but gets massive pretty quick, right? That's the idea here. You start by knocking out your smallest debt first, then take that payment and add it to the next one. It's like a debt demolition derby, and it feels awesome to see those numbers crash down.

- Next, consider the avalanche method. This one's for the folks who like playing the long game, focusing on the debts with the highest interest rates first. It might not give you the quick wins of the snowball method, but mathematically, you could save more in the long run. It's like choosing between a quick sprint or a marathon with a bigger medal at the end.

- Here's a curveball – negotiating your interest rates. Yep, you can actually call up your creditors and ask for a lower rate. Sounds a bit out there, but it's like haggling at a market; you never know until you try. Even a small percentage drop can save you big bucks over time, kind of like finding a hidden discount on your favorite scrubs.

- Don't overlook balance transfers, either. If you've got a credit card balance sitting at 20% interest, moving it to a card with a 0% introductory rate can give you a breather to pay it down. Just watch out for transfer fees and make sure you can beat the clock before the regular rates kick in. It's like getting a time-out in a game, but you've got to make your moves count.

- Lastly, there's the good old-fashioned budget overhaul. Dive into your spending and see where you can trim the fat. Maybe it's those fancy coffee runs or the cable package you never watch. Every dollar you redirect from spending to debt is like putting your money on a treadmill, working off the excess until you're in lean, mean financial shape.

So, there you have it, five more strategies to arm yourself in the battle against debt. Mix and match them to fit your style, and you'll be on your way to financial freedom before you know it.

3.3 The Power of Compound Interest

And now, for the grand finale: the mystical, magical power of compound interest. This is where things get really exciting. Imagine you're planting a money tree. Every year, it sprouts new branches (that's your interest), and then those branches sprout their own little branches (that's compound interest). Start early, and even a modest sapling can grow into a mighty oak. Albert Einstein (yeah, that Einstein) supposedly called compound interest the eighth wonder of the world. And who are we to argue with a genius? Invest early, keep at it, and you could be looking at a forest of wealth down the line.

To calculate compound interest, you can use this straightforward equation:

$$A = P(1 + r/n)^{nt}$$

Where:

A is the future value of the investment/loan, including interest.
P is the principal investment amount (the initial deposit or loan amount).
r is the annual interest rate (decimal).
n is the number of times that interest is compounded per year.
t is the time the money is invested or borrowed for, in years.

For example, if you're investing $500 a month at an annual interest rate of 12% compounded monthly for 5 years, the equation for each monthly investment becomes:

$$A = 500(1 + 0.12/12)^{12 \times 5}$$

Using this formula, you can calculate the future value for each monthly investment over 5 years, and then sum up all these values to get the total amount.

Compound interest is like a snowball rolling down a hill. At first, it starts off small and manageable. But as it keeps rolling, it picks up more snow, growing exponentially in size. That's your money with compound interest – starting small but expanding significantly over time.

Now, let's sprinkle in some numbers to see how this plays out in real life. Say you're setting aside $500 a month in an investment account with an average annual return of 7%. In 10 years, without adding any extra cash, that account could balloon to over $83,000. But here's where it gets wild. Let that sit for 30 years, and you're not just looking at double or triple. You're staring at a whopping $602,000! And that's without lifting a finger after your initial contributions.

What's crucial here is the 'time' factor. The earlier you start, the more dramatic the impact of the compound interest. It's like giving your money a longer runway to take off. A person who starts investing $300 a month at 25 could end up with over a million dollars by 65, assuming a 7% annual return. Wait until 35 to start, and you might have to settle for half of that, even with the same monthly contribution and return rate.

This isn't just about stashing cash in a savings account. The real magic happens when you invest in assets with higher returns, like stocks or mutual funds. Sure, they come with risks, but they also offer the potential for higher rewards, especially over the long haul.

So, the takeaway? Start early, stay consistent, and let the power of compound interest do the heavy lifting for you. It's one of the simplest, yet most effective strategies to grow your wealth over time. And the best part? It requires no special skills, just patience and discipline.

Let's explore how consistency plays a crucial role. Sticking to regular investments, even if they seem small at the outset, can lead to significant outcomes. The key is to make it a habit, like brushing your teeth or checking patient charts. This consistent approach allows your investments to grow steadily over time, benefiting from the market's ups and downs through a strategy known as dollar-cost averaging. Essentially, you're buying more when prices are low and less when prices are high, which can average your investment cost over time.

Another aspect to consider is the impact of reinvesting dividends. Many investments, especially stocks and mutual funds, pay out dividends.

Instead of pocketing these payments, reinvesting them back into your investment can supercharge your compound interest effect. This means your investment isn't just growing from the initial capital and its interest but also from the added boost of reinvested dividends, creating a multi-layered compounding effect.

Lastly, it's important to understand the role of risk and time horizon in leveraging compound interest. While younger investors might have the luxury to take on more risk for potentially higher returns, those closer to retirement might want to adopt a more conservative approach to protect their nest egg. Balancing risk with your time horizon ensures that you're not exposing yourself to unnecessary financial stress, while still making the most out of the compounding opportunities available to you.

By following these strategies—consistency, reinvesting dividends, and balancing risk—you can harness the full potential of compound interest, turning your financial goals from distant dreams into achievable realities.

And just like that, with the magic of compound interest, your financial future starts to look brighter, your retirement fund more robust, and your dreams more attainable. But why stop there? The journey to financial enlightenment doesn't end with mastering the art of letting your money work for you. Oh no, we're just getting started.

As we close the chapter on the foundational elements of your financial transformation, we stand at the threshold of a new adventure. Imagine standing at the peak of a mountain, gazing out at the vast landscape of opportunities that lay ahead. That's where we're headed next.

Buckle up, because in Chapter 4, we're diving headfirst into the art of painting your financial masterpiece. If compound interest is the canvas, strategic wealth design is the palette of colors you'll use to bring your vision to life.

Act II: Mastering the Art of Wealth

Chapter 4: Strategic Wealth Design

Welcome to the heart of our wealth-building adventure—Chapter 4. This is where we roll up our sleeves and get into the nitty-gritty of making your money work as hard as you do. We're talking about crafting a financial plan that's as tailored and precise as a treatment plan for a complex case. No fluff, just straight-up strategies and insights.

First up, we'll unpack the whole deal about diversifying your portfolio. It's like having a well-balanced diet for your investments to keep things healthy and resilient. We'll explore how spreading your investments across different types can shield you from unexpected downturns and keep your financial health in tip-top shape.

Then, we're going to tackle how you, the ever-busy doctor, can find smart and efficient ways to invest. Time's precious, and we want every minute you spend on your finances to count. We'll look into tools and techniques that streamline the process, assuring that your investment efforts are as efficient as an expertly managed OR.

Lastly, we'll navigate the roller coaster world of market fluctuations. Markets go up and down, but that doesn't mean your heart rate should follow suit. We'll cover strategies to keep your cool and stay the course, ensuring your financial goals don't get sidetracked by every bump in the market.

So, grab your favorite coffee, and let's get started. This chapter is all about empowering you with the knowledge and tools to design a wealth strategy that stands the test of time and lets you focus on what you do best—caring for others.

4.1 Designing a Diversified Portfolio

Let's chat about something super important but often misunderstood: diversification. Imagine you're preparing a multi-course meal for a dinner party. You wouldn't just serve one dish, right? If that dish doesn't turn out well, the whole dinner could be ruined. For us docs, it's like having different treatment plans for our patients. Some need meds, others need therapy, and a few might need surgery. Similarly, your investment portfolio needs a variety – a mix of stocks, bonds, real estate, and maybe even some alternative assets like art or gold. Did you know that a well-diversified portfolio can reduce risk and smooth out those investment ups and downs? That's right, it's not just about making more money; it's about protecting what you've got.

You know how in medicine, we don't rely on just one test or treatment to make all our decisions? Similarly, in investing, relying on just one type of asset is like navigating a tightrope without a safety net. Not the best idea, right?

You know how in medicine, we don't rely on just one test or treatment to make all our decisions? Similarly, in investing, relying on just one type of asset is like walking a tightrope without a safety net. Not the best idea, right? Just as a comprehensive approach is crucial in healthcare, diversification is key in investing.

So, here's the deal: when we talk about diversification, we're essentially spreading our investments across different assets. Why? Because different assets react differently to the same economic event. While stocks might take a hit during a downturn, bonds might hold steady or even gain value. And let's not forget about real estate or commodities like gold, which often march to the beat of their own drum.

Now, you might wonder, "How much should I invest in each?" Good question. Studies suggest that more than 90% of your portfolio's performance is determined by how you spread your investments, not just what specific stocks or bonds you pick. But there's no one-size-fits-all answer. It depends on your personal goals, your time horizon, and, importantly, how much risk you can stomach.

For instance, if you're closer to retirement, you might lean more towards bonds for their stability. But if retirement is a distant speck on the horizon, you might skew heavier towards stocks for growth. And don't forget to sprinkle in some real estate or REITs (Real Estate Investment Trusts) for good measure, plus maybe a dash of commodities or even some international investments to spice things up.

The key is regular check-ups, just like with our patients. Rebalancing your portfolio annually ensures it stays in line with your goals. Markets shift, and what was a perfect mix last year might need a tweak now.

So, there you have it. Building a diversified portfolio is like assembling a well-rounded medical team. Each specialist brings unique skills to the table, working together to keep your financial health in tip-top shape.

Consulting giant McKinsey reported that "total assets under management across private markets reached an all-time high of $9.8 trillion as of June 30, 2021, up from $7.4 trillion 12 months prior." Most industry experts agree this trend is likely to continue.

"The 60/40 Portfolio Is Delivering Its Worst Returns in a Century" — Wall Street Journal

When we're talking about mixing up your investments, it's all about not having all your money in just one spot. But hey, even some classic moves, like the old 60/40 split between stocks and bonds, are getting a bit shaky these days.

You might have heard folks swear by the 60/40 rule – that's where you keep 60% of your investments in stocks for growth and 40% in bonds for some steady income and a bit of a cushion. Well, turns out, that 2022 threw a curveball at that strategy. The Wall Street Journal pointed out on October 14, 2022, that this approach had its worst run in a century! Yep, you heard that right. Normally, bonds help soften the blow when stocks dip, but last year, that safety net kind of just... wasn't there. In fact, recent projections say that if someone continues the 60/40 strategy they can expect to make a little less than 3% a year on their portfolio over the next few years!

And it's not just about stocks and bonds anymore. The investment world is getting bigger and more varied. McKinsey's numbers show that private markets – that stuff like private equity, not your usual stocks – hit a whopping $9.8 trillion in assets by mid-2021.

So, what's the takeaway? It's clear that sticking to the same old might not cut it anymore. The game's changing, and it might be time to look beyond the usual and sprinkle in some different kinds of investments to keep your portfolio strong, no matter what the market throws your way.

4.2 Investment Strategies for the Busy Doctor

Now, let's talk about squeezing investment strategies into your insane schedule. I get it, between rounds, patients, and maybe catching a few Z's, who has the time? But here's a secret: it doesn't have to eat up your day. Ever heard of "set it and forget it" investments? Lots of doctors rally behind strong general partners that are running the investments for them, so they do the heavy lifting, and you don't have to. And with investing passively into pre-vetted opportunities, you're growing your wealth without even thinking about it.

Auto-Pilot Investing

First up, let's talk about putting your investments on auto-pilot. You're already managing a lot, so why not let technology lend a hand? Auto-investing is a game-changer. You set up a direct debit, and each month, a fixed amount goes straight from your paycheck into your investment account. Then when an opportunity pops up, like a business buyout, real estate development, medical office building, or other you can jump on it without having to scramble to find the cash. It's like having a personal assistant for your finances, ensuring you're consistently building wealth without lifting a finger. Studies show that regular, automatic investing can significantly increase your net worth over time, thanks to the magic of compounding.

Let's break down why it's such a smart move, especially for those with packed schedules:

- **Consistency is Key:** By automating your investments, you're committing to a consistent investment schedule. This consistency can be a major factor in long-term growth. Think about it – it's not about timing the market, but time in the market that counts.

- **Emotion-Free Investing:** One of the biggest benefits of auto-pilot investing is that it takes the emotion out of the equation. When you automate, you're less likely to make impulsive decisions based on market highs or lows. This can be a game-changer during turbulent times when emotions might otherwise lead you to make hasty decisions.

- **Harness the Power of Compounding:** With auto-pilot investing, every dollar you invest starts working for you, earning interest, and then that interest earns interest. Over time, this compounding effect can significantly boost your wealth growth.

- **Maximize Retirement Contributions:** For those eyeing an early retirement, auto-pilot investing can ensure you're maxing out your retirement accounts each year. Whether it's a 401(k), IRA, or another retirement vehicle, automating your contributions can help you hit those annual limits without having to scramble at year-end. If you want our guide on how to max out your retirement account and diversify it into alternatives just email us and we will send over some information.

- **Flexibility and Control:** While it's called "auto-pilot," you still have the controls. You can adjust your contribution amounts, pause them if necessary, or redirect them into different investment vehicles as your financial situation or goals change. This flexibility means you're not locked in, giving you peace of mind that you can adapt as needed.

By leaning into auto-pilot investing, you're leveraging a tool that can make a significant difference in your financial trajectory, especially when your day-to-day is already filled to the brim. It's about making your money work hard, so you don't have to sweat it.

Becoming a Limited Partner in a Syndication or Fund

Investing as a limited partner in a syndication or fund is an attractive option for those seeking low-maintenance investment opportunities. This approach allows you to invest in real estate or other assets without the burden of day-to-day management. Here's a step-by-step guide to becoming a limited partner:

1. **Understand the Basics:**

   - **Limited Partnership:** As a limited partner, you invest capital in a syndication or fund but are not involved in its daily operations. Your liability is limited to the amount of your investment.
   - **Syndication:** This involves pooling funds from multiple investors to purchase and manage large assets like real estate. A general partner (GP) manages the investment, while limited partners (LPs) provide the capital.

2. **Identify Investment Opportunities:**

   - **Research Sponsors:** Look for experienced sponsors (GPs) with a proven track record. Check their past performance, reputation, and alignment with your investment goals.
   - **Types of Investments:** Common syndications include multifamily properties, commercial real estate, and development projects. Funds can also target specific sectors like technology or healthcare.

3. **Evaluate the Deal:**

   - **Investment Summary:** Review the investment summary or prospectus. Understand the asset, location, market conditions, and the business plan.
   - **Financial Projections:** Analyze projected returns, cash flow, and exit strategy. Ensure the assumptions are realistic and align with your risk tolerance.

4. **Due Diligence:**

   - **Legal Documents:** Review the Private Placement Memorandum (PPM), operating agreement, and subscription agreement. Consider hiring an attorney to ensure you fully understand the terms.
   - **Background Check:** Verify the sponsor's credentials and track record. Look for any red flags or previous legal issues.

5. **Commit Your Capital**

   - **Minimum Investment:** Determine the minimum investment required. Syndications typically start at $50,000 or more.

- **Funding:** Transfer funds according to the instructions provided. Ensure you meet any deadlines for capital contributions.

6. Exit Strategy:

- **Investment Horizon:** Understand the expected holding period. Syndications often have a 5-10 year horizon.
- **Exit Mechanism:** Be aware of the exit strategy, whether it's through a sale, refinancing, or another liquidity event.

Benefits of Being a Limited Partner

- **Passive Income:** Enjoy regular distributions without active management responsibilities.
- **Diversification:** Gain exposure to assets like real estate that may not correlate directly with traditional stocks and bonds.
- **Professional Management:** Benefit from the expertise of experienced sponsors who handle the complexities of asset management.

Becoming a limited partner in a syndication or fund can be a rewarding way to diversify your investment portfolio while minimizing the time and effort required. By carefully selecting the right opportunities and conducting thorough due diligence, you can achieve solid returns with minimal involvement.

Let's unpack why these are such a smart choice for those of us with more on our plates than we can handle.

- **Cost-Effectiveness:** One of the biggest draws of index funds and ETFs is their cost efficiency. Unlike actively managed funds that charge higher fees for portfolio management, these low-maintenance options often come with minimal fees. This difference in expense ratios can save you a significant amount over the long haul. For instance, a 1% fee difference can add up to hundreds of thousands of dollars lost to fees over a 30-year investment period.

- **Diversification:** With just a single investment in an index fund or ETF, you're essentially buying a piece of the entire market or a specific sector. This built-in diversification reduces your risk because your investment isn't tied to the fortunes of a single company. It's like having a safety net that catches you if a few stocks in the fund fall.

- **Simplicity:** The beauty of these investment vehicles lies in their simplicity. There's no need to analyze individual stocks or constantly monitor market trends. Once you've invested, the fund takes care of the rest, tracking its respective index and making adjustments as needed without any effort on your part.

- **Tax Efficiency:** ETFs, in particular, are known for their tax efficiency due to their unique structure, which allows investors to buy and sell shares without triggering capital gains taxes. This can be a significant advantage for maintaining more of your earnings, especially for those in higher tax brackets.

- **Accessibility:** Both index funds and ETFs offer ease of access. You can start investing with relatively small amounts, making it possible to begin building your portfolio without waiting until you have a large sum to invest. Plus, with the rise of online brokerages, you can manage your investments from anywhere, anytime, which is perfect for the busy doctor on the go.

By leaning on these low-maintenance investment vehicles, you're not just making life easier for yourself; you're also setting up a solid, efficient foundation for long-term financial growth.

Time Blocking for Financial Check-Ins

Lastly, even the busiest doctor needs to check in on their financial health. Here's a pro tip: time blocking. Just like you might block out an hour for patient consultations or research, schedule a regular "financial check-up" for yourself. Once a quarter should do it. Use this time to review your investments, adjust your contributions, or simply reassure yourself that you're on the right track. A little focused time can make a big difference, ensuring your financial plan evolves with your life and career.

By integrating these strategies, you're setting up a robust, efficient system that grows your wealth in the background, letting you focus on what you do best: caring for your patients and enjoying your life outside the hospital.

4.3 Navigating Market Fluctuations

Market ups and downs can be scarier than a surprise midnight call to the ER. But here's the thing: they're part of the game. Capital markets have good days and bad ones, kind of like our patients. The key? Don't panic. It's like when you're faced with a crisis in the hospital; you stay calm, assess the situation, and act based on your training. In investing, that training tells us to stick to our plan, stay diversified, and keep in mind, it's about the long haul. Remember, historically, despite all its dips and dives, the market tends to go up over time. So, deep breaths, we've got this.

Market fluctuations can feel like a wild ride, but here's the kicker: they're normal, and believe it or not, manageable. It's all about perspective. When the capital market dips, it's not necessarily a crisis; it could just be a discount aisle in the world of investing. Historically, downturns have been followed by recoveries. In fact, after most market drops of 10% or more, what usually follows is a significant upswing within the next 12 months. The trick is to stay in the game, not sideline yourself in fear.

Also remember this… *losing is part of winning*, because every investment has some risk or volatility to it. You can't expect to win all the time, but the goal is to have your wins outweigh your losses, and compound those gains over time.

Think of it as your favorite TV medical drama – unexpected, full of twists, but always moving toward a resolution. It's not just about the thrill or the scare; it's about staying in your seat, gripping the safety bar, and riding through the highs and lows with a bit of excitement.

Sticking Through the Ups and Downs

Consider this: markets, much like patients, have good days and bad days. You wouldn't give up on a patient after a setback, right? Similarly, when the market dips, it's not bail-out time; it's when your commitment gets tested. And just like with patients, time tends to heal. Those who've stuck around have often seen their portfolios not just recover but grow stronger, kind of like how scars make us tougher.

Keeping Cool When It Heats Up

Lastly, let's talk about keeping your cool. Easier said than done, I know. But here's a trick: whenever the market goes on a wild ride, focus on something concrete – like why you invested in the first place or your goals, the same as focusing on your breathing during a stressful procedure. It centers you, keeps the panic at bay, and helps you make clear-headed decisions.

Staying the Course

When the capital market gets choppy, the worst move can often be sudden, reactive, emotional decisions. Think of your long-term financial plan as your north star, guiding you through the storm. A study showed that investors who stayed invested in the S&P 500 from 1999 to 2018, despite the ups and downs, saw an average annual return of about 5.6%. Those who tried to time the market and missed just a handful of the best days saw their returns slashed to 2% or less. The lesson? Time in the market beats timing the market, every time.

Patience in investing is like letting your money marinate. Markets will have their good days, bad days, and 'meh' days, but it's all part of the growth process. Investors who stayed put in the market between 1980 and 2018, even through the bad times, ended up with an average return of about 8.9% per year. Not too shabby, right?

Regular check-ins with your investments are not about second-guessing your choices every time the market sneezes. It's more like tuning a guitar – making small adjustments to keep it sounding sweet. A little tweak here and there ensures your portfolio still sings in harmony with your life's goals.

All this – the patience, the check-ins, the sticking to the plan – isn't just about avoiding losses. It's about setting yourself up for those wins that come with time. In the grand scheme, those market dips often look like tiny blips. Pull up a 30-year market chart, and those scary drops are barely noticeable in the long run. It's a reminder that today's panic can be tomorrow's footnote, especially if you're playing the long game, which, let's be honest, is what retirement planning is all about.

Wrapping up Chapter 4, we've navigated the essentials of crafting a diversified portfolio and strategies to keep your investments growing amidst your demanding schedule. But our journey doesn't end here. As we pivot to Chapter 5, we'll delve into an exciting realm often overlooked: diversifying your income beyond the hospital corridors. Stay tuned as we uncover the potential of side hustles tailored for the medical professional, blending passion with profit. Ready to explore how your expertise and interests can unlock new avenues of wealth? Let's turn the page.

Chapter 5: Diversifying Your Income Canvas

Welcome to Chapter 5, where we're diving into the art of diversifying your income. Think of your income as a canvas, and right now, it might be dominated by one color - your medical practice. It's time to add more hues and depth to this picture.

In this chapter, we'll explore three exciting avenues:

- **Exploring Side Hustles:** We'll kick things off with some inspiring tales of doctors who've moonlighted their way to extra income. From medical consulting to digital entrepreneurship, discover how your skills can open new doors beyond the clinic.

- **Passive Income Streams for Physicians:** Next, we delve into the world of passive income. Imagine earning without the constant time investment. We'll navigate through options like real estate and online courses, weighing the potential gains against the pitfalls.

- **Balancing Medicine and Entrepreneurship:** Finally, we tackle the big challenge - time management. Juggling a medical career with side projects isn't easy, but with the right strategies, it's more than possible. We'll share tips on how to manage this dual life without burning out.

By the end of this chapter, you'll have a palette of options to enrich your financial landscape and bring you closer to your dream of early retirement. Let's get started!

5.1 Exploring Side Hustles

First up, side hustles. They're not just for the Uber drivers and Etsy sellers of the world. Docs like us? We've got skills that can open doors you might not have even considered. Picture this: a colleague of mine started a medical blog. Fast forward a bit, and it's not just a blog; it's a go-to resource, pulling in ad revenue and sponsorship deals. And get this – nearly 37% of Americans have a side hustle. If they can do it, why not us?

Alright, let's chat more about these side hustles. You know, stepping into something like telemedicine as a side gig can be pretty neat. It's all about making the most of your time and expertise. You could be sitting in your PJs, sipping on some coffee, and still be giving valuable advice to someone in need, all thanks to the internet. It's kind of wild when you think about it. Plus, you're not adding a crazy commute or extra hours at the clinic. It's just you, your computer, and your brain doing what it does best.

Now, let's not overlook the whole online course gig. I mean, you've got knowledge that took years and a small fortune to acquire. Why not share that with folks willing to learn? You could whip up a course over a weekend, put it online, and boom, you've got a side hustle that keeps on giving. Every time someone clicks 'buy,' that's a little more in your pocket. And the best part? You do the work once, but the rewards keep rolling in.

And hey, if the digital world isn't your jam, there's always the more hands-on approach. Hosting workshops, giving talks at local schools, or even writing a book can be incredibly rewarding. Picture yourself standing in front of an eager crowd, sharing insights on wellness, nutrition, or stress management. It's not just about the extra cash; it's about making a difference and reaching out to the community in a whole new way. Plus, who wouldn't want to see their name on a book cover or be known as the go-to doc in town for health talks? It's a win-win, really.

Here are five points to consider when exploring side hustles:

- **Flexibility is Key:** Choose side hustles that fit your erratic schedule. Something you can pause and play as needed.

- **Leverage Your Expertise:** You're not just a doctor; you're a specialist in your field. Use that to your advantage in your side hustle.

- **Think Beyond Medicine:** Your skills as a communicator, leader, and problem-solver are valuable across various industries.

- **Start Small:** Don't go all-in from the get-go. Test the waters with minimal investment to see what resonates with you and your audience.

- **Network:** Connect with other professionals who are successfully managing side hustles. Their insights can be invaluable.

Remember, the goal here isn't to add more stress to your life but to enrich it, both intellectually and financially. With the right approach, your side hustle could not only boost your income but also provide a fulfilling outlet outside the medical world.

5.2 Passive Income Streams for Physicians

Now, onto the holy grail: passive income. It's the dream, right? Earning money while you sleep. Real estate is a classic route – think rental properties. Did you know that real estate has made up about 90% of the world's millionaires? But here's the catch: it's not all sunshine and rainbows. Being a landlord comes with its headaches. So, if you're thinking about diving in, maybe consider a property management company to keep the drama at bay.

Alright, let's keep rolling with the passive income chat. You know, online courses are kind of like planting a garden. You do the hard work upfront—planning the content, filming the videos, setting up the course—and then, once it's all setup and ready to go, you can pretty much sit back and watch it grow. Every time someone signs up for your course, that's a little bit of income without you having to do anything more. And with the e-learning market booming, there's a real appetite for quality content, especially from experts like us in the medical field.

Now, onto telemedicine. It's similar to having a side gig that fits around your life, rather than the other way around. You can log in and see patients from wherever you are, whether that's at home or on a beach somewhere (as long as you've got the internet). It's not 100% passive, sure, but it's a lot more flexible than traditional practice. Plus, with the industry growing like crazy, there's a lot of potential to tap into a patient base that values convenience and accessibility.

And then there's the whole world of creating something—whether it's a book, an app, or some revolutionary new medical tool. This is where you can get really creative. Write that book you've always talked about, or team up with a developer to bring your app idea to life. Once it's out there, it's out there. You could be kicking back, relaxing, and still making money every time someone downloads your app or buys your book. It's like setting up a bunch of little income streams that all flow into the big river of your bank account.

Here are five points to sum up some key takeaways:

- Online courses can turn your expertise into a global classroom, bringing in income with minimal ongoing effort.
- Telemedicine offers a more flexible approach to patient care, fitting consultations around your schedule.
- Writing a book or creating medical literature can establish you as an authority in your field and generate royalties.
- Developing a medical app taps into the ever-growing tech market, addressing needs within the healthcare sector.
- Patenting a new medical device or tool can lead to long-term financial rewards through licensing deals or sales.

So, what do you say? Ready to turn your expertise into an income engine that runs while you're doing... well, whatever you want? Let's make it happen!

5.3 Balancing Medicine and Entrepreneurship

Here's the big question: how do you juggle a demanding medical career with side gigs? It's all about finding that sweet spot. Time management is key. Block out time for your side hustle like you would for patient rounds or research. And remember, it's a marathon, not a sprint. Rome wasn't built in a day, and neither is a successful side business.

Setting Boundaries for Work and Play

Balancing your medical career with a side hustle starts with setting clear boundaries. Think of it as having an invisible line in your life; on one side is your role saving lives, and on the other, your entrepreneurial spirit thrives. It's crucial to decide when to wear which hat. For instance, dedicating weekends or specific evenings to your business can ensure that your side hustle doesn't encroach on your primary responsibilities. Remember, about 60% of small businesses are started at home, often in those spare moments outside the 9-5 grind.

Smart Time Management Strategies

Time is like a currency, especially for busy professionals like us. It's all about spending it wisely. Here are some strategies that can help:

- **Prioritize tasks:** Focus on what's urgent and important. Sometimes, what feels urgent isn't really that important in the grand scheme of things.

- **Use technology:** There are a ton of apps out there designed to streamline your schedule and to-do lists. Let technology be your assistant.

- **Delegate:** You don't have to do everything yourself. Whether it's in your medical practice or your side business, delegating tasks can free up a lot of time.

- **Batch tasks:** Group similar tasks together to improve efficiency. It's like doing all your grocery shopping in one go instead of multiple trips.

- **Set realistic goals**: Overcommitting is a surefire path to burnout. Set achievable goals that mesh with your medical career.

Leveraging Your Network

Your professional network can be a goldmine for your entrepreneurial ventures. About 85% of jobs are filled through networking, and the same principle applies when you're building a business. Connect with fellow physicians who've embarked on similar journeys. Their insights can be invaluable, helping you avoid common pitfalls and pointing you toward opportunities you might not have considered. Plus, your medical background can open doors in the healthcare sector that others might find closed.

Following Flexibility and Adaptability

If there's one thing medicine teaches us, it's to be adaptable. Your side hustle will need that same flexibility. Markets change, new trends emerge, and what worked yesterday might not work tomorrow. Stay nimble, be willing to learn, and don't be afraid to pivot your strategies if needed. It's said that the ability to adapt is one of the key traits of successful entrepreneurs.

Maintaining Work-Life Harmony

At the end of the day, it's not just about making more money. It's about enriching your life without sacrificing your well-being. Here are a few pointers to keep in mind:

- **Self-care is paramount:** Don't skimp on sleep, exercise, and downtime. Burnout is real, and prevention is better than cure.

- **Quality over quantity:** It's better to be fully present for a few things than to spread yourself too thin.

- **Remember your 'why':** Keep sight of why you started your entrepreneurial journey. It'll help you stay motivated.

- **Seek support:** Whether it's from family, friends, or mentors, having a support system can make all the difference.

- **Celebrate successes:** Take time to acknowledge your achievements, no matter how small. It's about the journey, not just the destination.

Balancing a demanding medical career with entrepreneurial ventures isn't easy, but it's definitely achievable. With the right strategies, boundaries, and mindset, you can build a fulfilling career both inside and outside the hospital.

Here are some real-life examples and case studies that highlight successful strategies in these areas:

Side Hustles

- **Real Estate Investment:** Real estate is a popular side hustle among various professionals, including doctors, due to its potential to generate extra income, diversify income sources, and build long-term wealth. Platforms like Arrived allow physicians to invest in income-producing properties with as little as $100, making real estate investment more accessible by removing traditional barriers like large down payments and the complexities of property management.

- **Starting a Podcast:** Many doctors have successfully launched podcasts to share their medical expertise, connecting with a global audience. For example, Dr. Joe Casciani's "Living to 100 Club" podcast discusses longevity and healthy aging, generating income through consultations and public speaking. Podcasts are relatively inexpensive to start and can be a scalable business model, appealing to a wide audience without significant incremental effort

- **Medical Writing and Consulting:** Leveraging your medical expertise to provide specialized content or consulting services is another effective side hustle. Whether it's contributing to medical websites, and journals, or offering regulatory writing services for pharmaceutical companies, medical writing can be a flexible and rewarding side gig.

Passive Income Streams

- **Telemedicine:** Offering telemedicine services is a natural extension of a physician's work, providing flexibility and the possibility of significant additional income. Physicians can engage in telemedicine through private practice, independently, or as contractors for telemedicine companies, with some positions offering malpractice insurance and other benefits.

- **Online Courses and Digital Products:** Creating and selling online courses based on your medical expertise is a powerful way to generate passive income. Once the course is developed, it can be sold repeatedly without much additional effort, potentially providing income for years.

- **YouTube and Digital Content Creation:** Establishing a YouTube channel to share health tips, medical knowledge, or wellness advice can be a lucrative passive income source. Successful medical YouTubers like Doctor Mike and Chubbyemu have built large followings, monetizing their content through ads, sponsorships, and affiliate marketing.

Balancing a demanding medical career with entrepreneurial ventures requires effective time management and strategic planning. Setting clear boundaries and dedicating specific times for your side hustles can help maintain this balance. Follow digital tools and platforms that offer flexibility, such as telemedicine or online course creation platforms, allowing physicians to work on their entrepreneurial projects without compromising their primary professional responsibilities.

These examples illustrate the variety of ways in which physicians can diversify their income and work towards financial independence, leveraging their unique skills and knowledge in the medical field. By carefully selecting and managing side hustles and passive income streams, doctors can achieve a balanced and fulfilling career while working towards early retirement.

As we close the chapter on diversifying your income, it's clear that stepping beyond the traditional confines of medicine can not only boost your earnings but also enrich your professional journey. Whether it's through blogging, real estate, or another passion-turned side hustle, each step you take adds vibrant strokes to your financial picture.

But diversification is just the beginning. The true art lies in fortifying these new income streams, ensuring they're not just fleeting successes but enduring pillars of your financial structure. It's about turning these ventures from mere sketches into lasting features of your income landscape, resilient and robust against the ebbs and flows of economic tides.

As we move forward, remember: your journey doesn't end with creating diverse income sources. The next step is to nurture and protect them, much like a curator preserves masterpieces in a gallery. It's about building a financial fortress where your wealth is not only generated but also safeguarded, ready to support your dreams of early retirement and beyond.

So, let's carry forward the entrepreneurial spirit from this chapter, using it as a foundation to build a secure, prosperous future. Here's to painting a financial masterpiece, one brushstroke at a time!

Chapter 6: The Fortress of Financial Solitude

Fellow life-savers! Welcome to Chapter 6, where we're about to roll up our sleeves and get down to the nitty-gritty of safeguarding your hard-earned wealth. Think of this chapter as your personal blueprint for constructing a financial fortress that's as sturdy and reliable as your medical advice.

We're diving into some critical areas that, honestly, don't get enough airtime in our busy lives. But just like we can't ignore the basics of health, we can't overlook these financial essentials either. We're talking about the kind of stuff that makes sure you keep enjoying those hard-earned dollars, even when life decides to throw a curveball or two your way.

First up, we'll tackle the beast known as disability insurance. I know it sounds a bit doom and gloom, but did you know that a whopping 1 in 4 of us will experience a disabling condition before we hit retirement? Yep, it's not just a tiny footnote in your contract; it's a real possibility. But don't worry, we'll guide you through choosing the right coverage, making sure you're as protected in life as you are in the operating room.

Next, we're going to talk about protecting your assets. It's not just about locking your doors at night; it's about creating a legal fortress around everything you've worked so hard for. With over 95% of the world's lawsuits filed in the good ol' US of A, it's no secret that doctors can be prime targets. But fear not, we'll show you how to shield your wealth from those legal arrows and keep your financial castle secure.

And finally, we'll delve into the world of estate planning. No, it's not just for the elderly or the ultra-rich. It's for anyone who wants to ensure their legacy is handled with the same care and precision they apply to their work. Surprisingly, 55% of Americans don't have a will or an estate plan in place. But not you, not after this chapter. We'll map out how to ensure your treasures, both financial and personal, are passed on exactly as you wish.

So, buckle up! We're about to embark on a journey to fortify your financial future, ensuring that what you've built withstands whatever life throws at it. Ready to build that fortress? Let's dive in!

6.1 The Essentials of Disability Insurance

Let's talk about something super important but often overlooked: disability insurance. Now, I know what you're thinking, "That's not going to happen to me, right?" But here's a startling fact: 1 in 4 of us will face a disabling condition before retirement. For doctors, that's not just a stat; it's a career game-changer. So, what's the move? Getting the right disability insurance is like having an unbeatable shield in your arsenal. It's not just any shield, though. You need one that's specifically crafted for the unique risks and rewards of the medical profession. Let's make sure you're covered, so if life throws a curveball, you're ready to catch it.

Getting the right disability insurance isn't just a checkbox on your to-do list; it's about wrapping your future in a safety net. So, what's the deal with choosing the right coverage? It's all about the details, like understanding the 'own occupation' clause, which is a big deal for us docs. This little gem means if you can't perform your specific medical duties, you still get benefits, even if you could work in another field.

And here's something you might not have thought about: the waiting period. It's like the countdown before your coverage kicks in. Shorter might sound better, but it can hike up your premiums. Finding that sweet spot is key.

Now, let's talk numbers because, let's face it, we love data. Did you know the cost of disability insurance can range from 1% to 3% of your income? It might sound like a chunk, but when you weigh it against the risk of losing your income for months, or even years, it's a no-brainer.

And don't forget about benefit period options. Some policies pay out until you're 65, but others offer shorter terms. Think about your financial runway and how long you'd need support to make a soft landing.

Lastly, let's touch on inflation protection. With the cost of living always on the rise, ensuring your benefits do the same is crucial. It's like giving your future self a raise, ensuring your benefits today will still hold their value years down the line.

- **Non-Cancellable vs. Guaranteed Renewable:** When choosing a policy, look out for 'non-cancellable' guarantees. This means your insurer can't cancel your policy or hike your premiums as long as you pay them. 'Guaranteed renewable' is good too, but it gives the insurer a bit more wiggle room to increase rates, as long as they do it for everyone under your policy category.

- **Partial Disability Benefits:** Life isn't always black and white, and neither is disability. Partial disability benefits are a safety net for those times when you can still work, but not at full capacity. It ensures a portion of your income is protected, even if you're not fully sidelined.

- **Future Increase Options:** Your income as a doctor is likely to grow over time, and your disability coverage should be able to keep up. Future increase options allow you to bump up your coverage amount as your salary increases, no medical check-up needed.

- **Mental Health Coverage:** It's a tough topic, but it's real, especially in high-stress jobs like ours. Some policies limit or exclude mental health-related disabilities. Make sure you know where your policy stands, so you're covered on all fronts.

- **Tax Considerations:** If you're paying your premiums with pre-tax dollars, your benefits might be taxable. On the flip side, using after-tax dollars for premiums could mean tax-free benefits. A little planning here can make a big difference in what you actually take home if you ever need to use the policy.

Lastly, make sure you have "own-occupation" disability insurance, also known as true or pure own-occupation. This is a long-term disability insurance that will pay benefits even if you are able to work in a capacity other than your current occupation. For example, an interventional cardiologist that injures hands will still receive benefits even if he or she decides to teach medical students for income. Another example: if an internist can't walk or do rounds in the hospital, but wants to earn income doing expert witness work on medmal cases, he or she would still get the disabilty benefit payments.

In wrapping up, diving into the world of disability insurance isn't just about signing on the dotted line. It's about understanding the ins and outs, from 'own occupation' clauses to inflation protection, ensuring you and your future are well-protected. After all, it's not just about if the unexpected happens, but being prepared when it does.

6.2 Protecting Your Assets

Next up, let's safeguard those hard-earned treasures of yours. Think of asset protection as building a fortress around your castle. Why? Well, in a world where 95% of the world's lawsuits happen in the U.S., doctors are like magnets for legal battles. Not the best kind of popularity, right? But fear not! With the right strategies, like trusts, insurance, and maybe even LLCs for your side gigs, you can keep your assets safe from sieges. It's all about making sure that what you've built stays in your kingdom, no matter the storms outside the castle walls.

Understanding Liability Coverage

First things first, liability coverage is your first line of defense. It's like having a moat around your castle. Here's why it's crucial:

- **Medical Malpractice Insurance:** Sure, it's a given, but are you really covered enough? The average payout for malpractice claims is creeping up, with some specialties seeing figures around $300,000. Check your policy limits!

- **Umbrella Policies:** These kick in where your other policies tap out. Considering that a single lawsuit can run into millions, an umbrella policy isn't just nice to have; it's a must.

- **Home and Auto:** Don't overlook these. A significant portion of personal lawsuits stem from incidents involving cars and homes. Ensuring these are solidly covered can save you a world of headaches.

Strategic Asset Ownership

How you own your assets can make a big difference in how protected they are. It's not just about owning; it's about smart owning.

- **Titling Assets Wisely:** Did you know that assets owned jointly with your spouse are often shielded from individual lawsuits? It's a simple tweak with big implications.

- **Use of Trusts:** Trusts aren't just for the ultra-rich. They can protect your assets from creditors, lawsuits, and even estate taxes, keeping more of what you've earned in your pocket.

- **Retirement Accounts:** IRAs and 401(k)s enjoy protection under federal law, with ERISA-covered plans being virtually lawsuit-proof. Maxing these out isn't just good for your retirement; it's smart for asset protection.

Incorporating Your Practice

If you're running your own practice, how it's structured can significantly impact your personal financial vulnerability.

- **LLCs and S-Corps:** These structures can shield your personal assets against business debts and lawsuits. It's about separating your business battles from your personal finances.

- **Professional Liability Insurance:** Beyond malpractice, ensure you're covered for the business side of things. A slip and fall at your office shouldn't jeopardize your personal savings.

- **Regular Compliance Reviews:** Keeping your business in line with legal and regulatory standards can prevent a multitude of issues. An ounce of prevention is worth a pound of cure, as they say.

By fortifying these aspects of your financial life, you're not just protecting your assets; you're securing your peace of mind and ensuring that your hard work continues to serve you, your family, and your legacy, no matter what comes your way.

Alright, let's take a moment to look at a real-world example that'll help make sense of all this financial talk. Imagine there's this company called "ABC Private Equity," and they're handling a big pot of money, say $1 billion. Now, they don't do this for free. They charge a fee, of 2% every year, just for managing this money. So, every year, they're pocketing $20 million just from fees. Over five years, that's a cool $100 million. Pretty sweet deal, right?

Now, let's say you decide to get in on this action. You put $1 million into the company, not into the fund they manage, but directly into the company itself, kind of like becoming a mini-owner. Because of how they've set things up, this move starts paying you back right away. You could be looking at an extra $50,000 to $100,000 every year, just from your $1 million investment.

This example shows why it's smart to think about where you're putting your money. It's not just about saving; it's about investing wisely and maybe even getting into the game of managing other people's money. This way, you're not just watching your money grow; you're actively making it grow faster.

6.3 Estate Planning for Physicians

Lastly, let's chat about estate planning. I know, I know, it sounds like something only the ultra-wealthy need to worry about. But here's a reality check: 55% of Americans pass away without a will or estate plan. For doctors, who've spent a lifetime building a legacy, that's like leaving the fate of your kingdom to chance. Estate planning is your map to ensure that your treasures - be it your wealth, your practice, or even your values - are passed on exactly how you wish. It's not just about the here and now; it's about scripting the legacy you leave behind.

Estate planning might seem like a heavy topic, but it's really about ensuring that everything you've worked so hard for goes exactly where you want it to when you're no longer here. It's about taking control and making decisions that reflect your wishes, not leaving things up to state laws or courts, which might not align with your desires. Think about it: you've spent countless hours in the OR, the clinic, and beyond, building a life and a legacy. Estate planning is how you protect that legacy and ensure it supports the people and causes that you care about the most.

Now, let's dive into the nuts and bolts. A solid estate plan for a physician isn't just a will – though that's a crucial part of it. It's a collection of legal tools and directives that together, paint a clear picture of your wishes. For example, a trust can be a game-changer, especially for those with a bit more complexity in their financial or family situation. It can help manage your assets more efficiently and even keep things private and out of probate court. Then there's the power of attorney – both for finances and healthcare. These ensure that if you're ever unable to make decisions for yourself, someone you trust is legally appointed to do so on your behalf.

But estate planning isn't a "set it and forget it" kind of deal. Life changes, and so should your estate plan. Maybe you're welcoming a new member to the family, or perhaps there's been a change in your professional life, like joining a new practice or even starting your own. These milestones are the perfect time to revisit your plan. Ensuring it's up-to-date and there's no ambiguity about your intentions, providing you and your loved ones with peace of mind.

Here are five key points to keep in mind when it comes to estate planning for physicians:

- **Wills and Trusts:** These are the cornerstones of any estate plan. A will covers the basics of who gets what, but a trust can offer more control over how and when your assets are distributed.

- **Advanced Directives:** Clearly outline your healthcare wishes in case you're unable to communicate them yourself. It's not just for the elderly; anyone can face a sudden medical crisis.

- **Guardianship:** If you have children, deciding on guardianship is crucial. It ensures they're cared for by people you trust, in line with your parenting values and wishes.

- **Tax Planning:** Estate taxes can take a big bite out of what you leave behind. Strategic planning can help minimize this impact, ensuring more of your legacy goes to your loved ones.

- **Regular Reviews:** Life's only constant is change. Regularly reviewing and updating your estate plan ensures it always matches your current situation and future goals.

Estate planning is more than just legal documents; it's an act of love and responsibility. It's how you ensure that the wealth and legacy you've built serves your loved ones and reflect your values, even when you're not around to make those choices yourself.

Let's dive into some real-life scenarios that highlight the importance of estate planning for physicians, keeping it light and relatable:

Dr. Smith's Trust Fund Triumph

Dr. Smith, a pediatrician, set up a trust fund not just to manage her wealth, but to ensure her two kids' education was covered, no matter what. When she unexpectedly passed away, the trust fund kicked in, covering tuition, books, and even dorm fees for both kids through college and med school. It was like she was still supporting them every step of the way.

Dr. Jones and the Guardianship Game-Changer

Emergency medicine doc, Dr. Jones, never thought he'd be in a situation where he couldn't make decisions for himself. But after a skiing accident left him incapacitated for months, the guardianship decisions he'd laid out in his estate plan ensured his brother, who shared his values and understood his wishes, stepped in. This move kept his personal and financial matters running smoothly while he recovered.

The Unexpected Tax Tackle by Dr. Patel

Dr. Patel, a renowned cardiologist, was all about saving lives but didn't think much about saving on taxes. After her passing, her estate was hit with significant taxes, a chunk of which could have been avoided with some strategic planning. Her colleagues learned from this, taking a closer look at their estate plans to include tax-saving strategies, ensuring more of their hard-earned money went to their families and less to the taxman.

Dr. Lee's Legacy Locked In

Dr. Lee, a passionate oncologist, dedicated his life to cancer research. Through his estate plan, he allocated a portion of his assets to fund ongoing research projects, ensuring his legacy lived on in the fight against cancer. His thoughtful planning meant that even in his absence, his commitment to making a difference continued, funding breakthroughs and supporting new researchers in the field.

Dr. Garcia's Guardianship Go-To

Pediatric surgeon Dr. Garcia chose her sister to be the guardian of her children, clearly outlining this in her estate plan. When an unexpected tragedy struck, her sister stepped in seamlessly to care for the kids, just as Dr. Garcia would have wanted. This foresight prevented any custody battles or family disputes, keeping the focus on the children's well-being during a tough time.

Each of these stories underscores the power and impact of thoughtful estate planning, ensuring that even when life throws curveballs, your wishes and legacy carry on just as you'd hoped.

As we wrap up this chapter on fortifying your financial defenses, remember: safeguarding your wealth isn't just a one-time task; it's an ongoing journey. With the right disability insurance, you're not just protecting your income; you're ensuring your peace of mind. By securing your assets against unforeseen legal battles, you're not merely building walls; you're creating a sanctuary for your hard-earned wealth. And with thoughtful estate planning, you're not just drafting documents; you're scripting the legacy you'll leave behind.

As we turn the page from safeguarding our wealth to optimizing it, Chapter 7 opens up a new realm of possibilities. The Art of Tax Efficiency is more than just finding ways to reduce your tax bill—it's about strategically aligning your financial decisions with tax laws to maximize your wealth's potential. Think of it as fine-tuning the defenses of your financial fortress to not only withstand sieges but to thrive and prosper. Stay tuned as we delve into the tactics and strategies that will elevate your financial savvy to new heights, ensuring your wealth works as hard for you as you did for it.

Chapter 7: The Art of Tax Efficiency

Welcome to Chapter 7. We're about to tackle taxes. I know, just hearing the word "taxes" might make you want to run the other way, but hang tight. Understanding this stuff could be a game-changer for your early retirement plans.

In this chapter, we're hitting up three big topics that could really make a difference in your wallet:

Tax Planning for High Earners: We're kicking off with some smart strategies. If you're earning a solid income as a doc, you're probably paying a chunk of it in taxes, right? Well, it doesn't have to be quite so painful. We'll look into ways you might be able to keep more of that hard-earned money instead of handing it over to the taxman.

Understanding Tax-Advantaged Accounts: Then, we're going to break down those accounts like 401(k)s, IRAs, and HSAs that come with some sweet tax breaks. It's like discovering a secret shortcut that lets you keep more of your cash safe from taxes. For example, just by maxing out your 401(k), you could protect up to $19,500 of your income from taxes every year. Pretty cool, right?

Tax-Efficient Investing: And last, we'll talk about how to make your investments a bit smarter when it comes to taxes. Not all investments are taxed in the same way, and knowing how to play that can mean more money stays with you. Like, did you know that if you hold onto some investments for over a year, you could pay a lot less tax on the profits?

So, let's jump in! By the end of this chapter, you'll have some solid tax tips up your sleeve, helping you keep more of your money and getting you closer to that dream of retiring early. Let's get started!

7.1 Tax Planning for High Earners

Alright, high earners, listen up. You're in a unique club where Uncle Sam is particularly interested in your earnings. Did you know that folks in the top income brackets can end up paying almost 37% in federal taxes alone? That's a big chunk of your hard-earned cash. But fear not, there are legit ways to navigate this. Think of tax planning like a chess game where knowing the moves can keep more of your money in your pocket. We're talking about strategies such as tax-loss harvesting or smartly timing your income and deductions. It's all about playing the game with the rules in your favor.

Advanced Strategies for High-Income Docs

When you're pulling in those big doctor bucks, the tax bite can feel more like a chomp. But, there are strategies to soften the blow.

Smart Income Timing

- **Year-End Bonuses:** Consider asking your employer to defer any year-end bonuses to the next tax year, especially if you anticipate being in a lower tax bracket.

- **Retirement Contributions:** Max out your retirement contributions to reduce your taxable income. The more you put away, the less the IRS gets now.

- **Business Expenses:** If you have any control over your practice or side gigs, time your expenses so you can deduct them in higher-income years.

- **Harvesting Losses:** Got underperforming investments? Selling them to realize losses can offset gains in other areas of your portfolio.

- **Charitable Contributions:** Bigger donations in high-income years can mean more significant deductions. Consider donor-advised funds to manage the timing of your charitable giving.

So, think about it like this: If you could choose when to pay less tax, you'd take that chance, right? That's what smart income timing is all about. It's like deciding to eat dessert first because you know the main course is going to be super filling later on. If you've got a bonus coming up, maybe chat with your boss about pushing it to next year, especially if you think you'll be in a lower tax bracket. It's all about making the calendar work for you, not against you.

And when it comes to investments, it's like having a garden where some plants need trimming at the right time to bloom better next season. That's tax-loss harvesting. You let go of the investments that aren't doing great, use those losses to balance out the wins, and your tax bill gets a bit lighter. It's turning a not-so-great situation into a win for your wallet.

Utilizing Tax-Deferred Accounts

- **Traditional IRA:** Even if you're above the deduction limit, non-deductible contributions to a Traditional IRA can still grow tax-deferred.

- **SEP and SIMPLE IRAs:** For self-employed docs or those with side hustles, these accounts offer higher contribution limits, reducing your taxable income.

- **Health Savings Account (HSA):** Contributions are tax-deductible, and funds can grow and be withdrawn tax-free for qualified medical expenses.

- **Deferred Compensation Plans:** If available, these plans allow you to defer a portion of your income to future years, potentially lowering your current tax bracket.

- **Real Estate Investments:** Investing in real estate can provide tax-deferred growth and deductions like depreciation, which can offset income.

Alright, tax-deferred accounts are basically your financial hideaway spots. You're putting money aside, and the taxman has to wait outside until you're ready to use it. Think of it like stashing your favorite snacks in a secret drawer, and you only share them when you're really ready.

For us high earners, these accounts are like VIP clubs where our money can chill out and grow without getting nibbled away by taxes every year. Whether it's a 401(k), an IRA, or something more specific like an HSA, each contribution is like sending your dollars to a tax vacation. And who doesn't love a good vacation, right?

Strategic Asset Location

- **Taxable vs. Tax-Advantaged:** Place high-growth investments in Roth accounts where withdrawals are tax-free, and income-producing assets in traditional, tax-deferred accounts.

- **Municipal Bonds:** The interest from these bonds is often exempt from federal taxes, making them an attractive option for taxable accounts.

- **Index Funds and ETFs:** These tend to be more tax-efficient and are better suited for taxable accounts due to lower turnover rates.

- **Real Estate Crowdfunding:** For accredited investors, these can offer tax-advantaged income through depreciation and other real estate-specific deductions.

- **Tax-Managed Funds:** These funds are designed to minimize tax liabilities and are ideal for high earners looking to optimize their taxable account investments.

Now, onto where you keep your investments. Imagine you've got a toolbox. You wouldn't put a delicate paintbrush in with the heavy hammers, right? That's the idea behind strategic asset location. You're matching your investments with the right type of account to keep them safe from unnecessary taxes.

Putting your growth-focused investments, like stocks, in a Roth IRA is like storing your fancy dinnerware in the top cabinet — it's safe, and when you take it out, there's no extra cost. Then, for the regular accounts, think about using them for stuff like municipal bonds, which are already tax-friendly, kind of like keeping your everyday dishes on an easy-to-reach shelf.

By diving deep into these strategies and really understanding the nuances of each, you can start to build a more tax-efficient portfolio that aligns with your income level and financial goals. Remember, the goal here isn't just to reduce taxes for the sake of it but to ensure that every dollar you save on taxes is working as hard for you as you did to earn it.

7.2 Understanding Tax-Advantaged Accounts

Now, let's dive into the treasure trove of tax-advantaged accounts. If you're not already besties with accounts like 401(k)s, IRAs, and HSAs, it's time to get acquainted. These aren't just acronyms to glaze over. They're your secret weapons against tax erosion. For example, maxing out your 401(k) can shield a whopping $19,500 (or $26,000 if you're 50 or older) from taxes each year. And with IRAs, you've got another opportunity to save $6,000 annually ($7,000 for the 50+ crowd). These accounts are like financial bunkers, sheltering your money from taxes as it grows.

Let's get a bit more into the weeds, but I promise to keep it light. Think of these accounts as your financial VIP lounge, where your money gets to chill and grow without the constant tax nibbles. It's pretty sweet.

First up, Health Savings Accounts (HSAs). If you've got a high-deductible health plan, you're eligible for one of these bad boys. Here's the kicker: contributions are tax-deductible, the money grows tax-free, and if you use it for qualified medical expenses, it's tax-free coming out too. Triple tax advantage, anyone? And after you turn 65, you can use HSA funds for anything, not just medical expenses, though you'll pay regular income tax on non-medical withdrawals. It's like a secret retirement account most people overlook. In 2021, you could sock away up to $3,600 as an individual or $7,200 for family coverage. Not too shabby, right?

Then there's the world of 529 plans, which are like a turbocharged savings account for education expenses. You put money in, and it grows tax-free. Use it for tuition, books, or even some room and board costs, and you won't pay a dime in taxes on those withdrawals. Some states even give you a tax break on your contributions. It's a fantastic way to ensure that education, for you or your kids, doesn't become a financial burden down the line. Plus, with education costs soaring, getting a head start on saving can make all the difference.

Lastly, let's chat about Roth IRAs and Roth 401(k)s. These accounts are all about paying taxes now to avoid them later. You contribute after-tax dollars, but once that money is in, it's like a tax-free growth party. And when it's time to retire, you can make withdrawals without owing a cent to Uncle Sam on those gains. For young docs or those in lower tax brackets now but expecting to be in higher ones later, Roth options are golden. It's like locking in your tax rate today, betting that it's a bargain compared to what's coming down the road. And with Roth IRAs, there's also a bit of flexibility with early withdrawals, making it a bit of a Swiss Army knife in your financial toolkit.

So, there you have it. Tax-advantaged accounts aren't just a piece of the puzzle; they're the corner pieces that help everything else fall into place. Leveraging them can seriously amplify your financial growth, making that dream of early retirement more than just a dream. It's about putting your money to work in the smartest way possible, keeping more of it in your pocket and less in Uncle Sam's.

7.3 Tax-Efficient Investing

Investing with taxes in mind is like choosing the right tool for the job – it just makes everything smoother. Not all investments are taxed equally. Long-term capital gains, for instance, enjoy lower tax rates as compared to your regular income. So, if you're holding onto assets like stocks or mutual funds for more than a year, you're looking at a tax rate that maxes out at 20% – way lower than the top income tax bracket. And let's not forget about tax-efficient funds, like index funds or ETFs, which tend to generate fewer taxable events, keeping more money in your portfolio and less in the taxman's pocket.

Let's break it down even further. Investing isn't just about picking winners; it's about keeping as much of those winnings as possible after taxes.

Choosing the Right Account for the Right Investment

Think of your investments like plants. Some thrive in the sun; others prefer the shade. Stocks, for example, are like your sun-loving plants. Held in taxable accounts, they benefit from lower long-term capital gains rates, especially if you're holding them for over a year. Now, your bonds are a different story. They're like your shade plants, preferring the shelter of tax-deferred accounts like IRAs or 401(k)s, where their interest payments won't be taxed each year. This strategy, called asset location, is all about matching your investments with the most tax-friendly environment.

Choosing the Right Account for the Right Investment," it's like putting each piece of your financial puzzle in just the right spot. Let's break it down:

- **Taxable Accounts for Growth Stocks:** When we're talking growth stocks, think of them as your long-term players. They're in it for the growth, not so much for the dividends. Since they might not pay out much now, but could be worth a lot more later, having them in a taxable account makes sense. Why? Because when you sell them down the line, after they've hopefully grown a bunch, you'll pay the long-term capital gains tax, which is usually lower than regular income tax rates. And if you've held onto them for over a year, you're looking at a tax rate that could be as low as 0%.

- **Retirement Accounts for Interest-Bearing Investments:** Bonds and CDs, they're your steady eddies, paying out interest regularly. But that interest gets taxed like regular income, which can be a bummer if you're in a high tax bracket. Tucking these into a retirement account like an IRA or 401(k) shields that interest from taxes year after year, which can really add up.

- **Roth IRAs for High-Growth Potential Investments:** Got an investment you think might be a home run? Consider placing it in a Roth IRA. Here's the deal: with a Roth, you pay taxes upfront, but withdrawals in retirement are tax-free. So, if that investment hits it big, all those gains are yours to keep, no tax strings attached.

- **HSAs for Healthcare-Related Investments:** Health Savings Accounts (HSAs) are a bit of a triple threat in a good way. Your contributions are tax-deductible, the growth is tax-free, and if you use the funds for medical expenses, those withdrawals are tax-free too. If you're eyeing investments related to healthcare, an HSA could be a perfect match.

- **529 Plans for Education-Focused Investments:** Saving for education? 529 Plans are like the VIP section for education savings. You might not get a federal tax break on contributions, but many states give you a deduction or credit. Plus, the money grows tax-free, and if you use it for qualified education expenses, you won't pay taxes on withdrawals either.

By matching up your investments with the right accounts, you're not just investing wisely; you're investing strategically. It's all about making the tax rules work in your favor, so more of your money stays where it belongs – with you.

Smart Moves with Mutual Funds

Mutual funds can be a bit chatty when it comes to taxes. They're constantly buying and selling within the fund, which can lead to capital gains distributions that you get taxed on, even if you haven't sold the fund yourself. But here's a pro tip: Index funds and ETFs tend to be quieter. They have lower turnover rates, meaning they buy and sell less frequently, leading to fewer taxable events. And when it comes to year-end, they often have lower capital gains distributions, keeping your tax bill more manageable.

Continuing our chat on smart moves with mutual funds, let's zero in on some nifty strategies to keep things tax-efficient:

- **Look for Low Turnover Rates:** Mutual funds that buy and sell a lot can rack up capital gains, which land in your lap as taxable distributions. Opting for funds with low turnover rates means fewer buy/sell activities, leading to fewer capital gains handed down to you. It's like choosing a car that needs less gas; it just keeps your costs lower.

- **Consider Tax-Managed Funds:** Some mutual funds are designed with tax efficiency in mind. Managers of these funds use strategies to minimize taxable distributions, like holding onto investments longer to qualify for long-term capital gains or offsetting gains with losses. It's like having a financial mechanic tune your investments to run more efficiently on the tax track.

- **Timing Matters:** If you're eyeing a mutual fund, check when it distributes capital gains. Buying right before a distribution means you'll get hit with a tax bill for gains you didn't even enjoy. It's akin to hopping on a bus and immediately getting charged for the previous passenger's full ride.

- **Eye the Expense Ratio:** This is the annual fee the fund charges as a percentage of your investment. Lower expense ratios mean more of your money stays invested and has the potential to grow. It's like choosing a bank with lower fees; over time, the savings can really add up.

- **Use Dividend-Efficient Funds for Taxable Accounts:** Funds focusing on qualified dividends can be more tax-efficient in taxable accounts, thanks to the favorable tax treatment of these dividends. It's a bit like choosing groceries that are on sale; you're just getting more bang for your buck.

By keeping these points in mind, you can navigate the mutual fund landscape a bit more smoothly, keeping an eye on both growth and tax efficiency. It's all about making your investments work hard for you, without giving Uncle Sam a bigger slice of the pie than necessary.

The Beauty of Tax-Loss Harvesting

Let's talk about turning lemons into lemonade, or in our case, turning investment losses into tax wins. Tax-loss harvesting is about selling investments that are at a loss and using those losses to offset other gains or even some of your regular income. Say you've got some stocks that didn't perform well, and you're sitting on a loss. You can sell those stocks, "harvest" the losses, and then use those losses to balance out other gains you've made. The cool part? If your losses are more than your gains, you can use up to $3,000 of those losses to reduce your regular income every year. It's like a silver lining playbook for your investments.

Let's really break down why it's such a neat trick in your financial toolkit:

- **Timing is Everything:** With tax-loss harvesting, timing can play a big role. You don't have to wait until the end of the year to do this. In fact, keeping an eye out for opportunities throughout the year can help you react to market dips more effectively. This proactive approach ensures you're not leaving tax-saving opportunities on the table.

- **The Wash-Sale Rule:** Now, there's a catch called the wash-sale rule. It says if you sell a stock at a loss and buy the same or "substantially identical" stock within 30 days before or after the sale, you can't claim that loss for tax purposes. But here's a workaround: you can still sell a losing stock and then buy a different stock that serves a similar role in your portfolio, keeping your investment strategy on track without missing out on the tax benefits.

- **Rebalancing Your Portfolio:** Tax-loss harvesting offers a great chance to rebalance your portfolio. Let's say some of your investments have strayed from your target allocation. By selling off the underperformers to harvest losses, you can reinvest in areas that align better with your goals, effectively hitting two birds with one stone: optimizing your portfolio and saving on taxes.

- **Carryover Advantage:** If your harvested losses exceed your gains, or you have more than the $3,000 you can deduct from your ordinary income in a year, no worries! You can carry over unused losses to future tax years indefinitely. This carryover can be a strategic reserve you can tap into for offsetting future gains or income, making it a gift that keeps on giving.

- **It's Not Just for the Big Players:** Some folks think tax-loss harvesting is only for the wealthy, but that's not the case. Even if you're just starting out or if your portfolio isn't massive, you can still use this strategy. Every little bit helps, and reducing your taxable income by even a small amount can lead to savings that add up over time, especially when you reinvest those savings.

Remember, tax-loss harvesting is about making strategic moves, not just random sell-offs. It's a way to turn the market's inevitable ups and downs to your advantage, smoothing out your tax bill and potentially boosting your investment returns over the long haul. So, keep an eye on your portfolio and consider making tax-loss harvesting a regular part of your financial check-up.

Here are some practical approaches and case studies drawn from experts in the field:

Municipal Bonds for Tax-Free Income: High earners can benefit significantly from investing in municipal bonds, which offer tax-exempt interest income. This can be particularly advantageous for those in higher tax brackets seeking to reduce their taxable income. For example, investing in a Vanguard Tax Exempt Municipal Bond ETF, as highlighted by Barbara Friedberg, can provide competitive returns with the added benefit of tax efficiency (Barbara Friedberg Personal Finance).

Tax-Efficient Mutual Funds and Index Funds: Selecting mutual funds and index funds that are managed with tax efficiency in mind can help minimize capital gains taxes. Funds with low turnover rates, such as the Vanguard Tax-Managed Balanced Fund, are designed to reduce taxable distributions, thereby enhancing after-tax returns for investors (Barbara Friedberg Personal Finance).

Leveraging Opportunity Zones: High-income earners can also look into investing in Opportunity Zones, which offer the potential to defer and possibly eliminate capital gains taxes on investments made in designated economically distressed areas. This requires careful due diligence but can be a powerful strategy for tax-efficient growth.

Income Splitting and Trusts: Another strategy is income splitting, which involves distributing income among family members to take advantage of lower tax brackets. Trusts can also be used to manage and protect assets while providing potential tax benefits. This approach requires careful planning and legal advice to ensure compliance with tax laws (Eva Cox).

Charitable Donations and Tax Deductions: Donating to charitable organizations not only supports worthy causes but also offers tax deductions. High earners can donate appreciated assets to charities, avoiding capital gains taxes on the appreciation while potentially receiving a tax deduction for the market value of the asset (Eva Cox).

Real Estate Exemptions and Rollovers: High earners involved in real estate can use exemptions and rollovers, such as the 1031 exchange, to defer capital gains taxes on property sales. This strategy allows investors to reinvest proceeds from real estate sales into new properties without immediate tax implications (Eva Cox).

In the context of real estate investment, the historical performance of this asset class provides a compelling narrative for its inclusion in a diversified portfolio. Over the past four decades, real estate investors have experienced a favorable environment, largely attributed to the consistent decline in interest rates from their peak in 1981 at just under 16 percent. This prolonged period of decreasing rates has propelled asset prices upward, with real estate standing out as a notable beneficiary. Despite the brief disruption during the Global Financial Crisis, the sector has demonstrated remarkable resilience and growth. In fact, the year 2021 marked a significant milestone, with real estate delivering its strongest returns since the pre-2008 era, even amidst the unexpected challenges of the COVID pandemic.

These insights and strategies underscore the importance of a nuanced approach to investing, particularly for high earners seeking to maximize their financial potential while navigating the complexities of tax regulations. By integrating these tax-efficient strategies and considering the historical performance and future prospects of various asset classes, investors can make informed decisions that align with their financial objectives and risk preferences.

There are a few other ways to slash your taxes that are a bit more complex than what we cover in this book, such as specific trust structures, 1031 exchanges, and more, that can even eliminate taxes in certain categories altogether. To get a copy of our top 20 Tax Strategies that are often missed, use the QR Code below and we will send it right over:

Conclusion: Mastering the Tax Game

And that, my fellow physicians, is how you turn the tax game from a dreaded chore into a strategic advantage. By now, you should feel a bit more like a tax ninja, armed with the knowledge to protect your wealth and steer it towards growth rather than letting it get nibbled away by taxes.

Remember, it's not just about how much you make but how much you keep that counts. Those tax-advantaged accounts aren't just bureaucratic red tape; they're golden opportunities to build your wealth under a protective shield. And when it comes to investing, choosing the right vehicles can mean the difference between a smooth ride and a bumpy one when tax season rolls around.

Now, as we wrap up this chapter on tax efficiency, let's peek over the horizon at what's next: Chapter 8: Envisioning Early Retirement. Think of tax efficiency as laying down the tracks for the retirement train you're going to ride. In the next chapter, we'll dive into how to build the engine and fuel it to get you to your destination of early retirement. We'll explore crafting a retirement plan that's not just a dream but a tangible, achievable reality, giving you the freedom to enjoy life on your terms sooner rather than later.

So, take a moment to pat yourself on the back for tackling the tax beast. With this newfound knowledge, you're one step closer to that early retirement beach, where the only numbers you'll need to crunch are the SPF of your sunscreen and the perfect time to catch the sunset. Let's roll up our sleeves and turn those retirement dreams into plans. See you in Chapter 8!

Chapter 8: Envisioning Early Retirement

Welcome to Chapter 8, where we're diving headfirst into the dream zone: early retirement. Now, I know what you're thinking – retirement talk already? But trust me, it's never too early to start envisioning those golden years, especially when you've been in the grind as long as we have.

In this chapter, we're going to break down the big three essentials to making your retirement not just a possibility, but a fabulous reality. First up, we'll tackle how to figure out exactly what you'll need to live that dream retirement life. Spoiler alert: it's probably more than you think, but don't sweat it; we've got strategies!

Next, we'll chart the course to financial independence. It's like mapping out the most epic road trip, but instead of hitting the open road, you're securing your future freedom. With less than half of docs feeling good about their retirement game plan, we're here to boost those numbers.

And finally, we'll talk about making your hard-earned cash last. Because what's the point of retiring early if you're going to spend your days stressing about every penny? We'll explore smart withdrawal strategies to keep you living comfortably, from your first day of retirement to your 100th birthday bash.

So, buckle up! We're about to make early retirement less of a daydream and more of a game plan.

8.1 Calculating Retirement Needs

Hey there, future retiree! Let's talk turkey about what you'll need to hang up that stethoscope for good. Picture your dream retirement. Maybe it's a cozy beach house, globe-trotting, or just quality time with the grandkids. Got it? Great! Now, let's crunch some numbers. On average, folks spend about 70-80% of their pre-retirement income to keep the good times rolling. But hey, you're not average, right? Considering doctors' lifestyles, bumping that to 90% might not be overkill. Remember, it's not just about covering bills; it's about living your retirement dream.

To really nail down what you'll need in retirement, we've got to cover a few bases. Think of it as mapping out the trip of a lifetime. You wouldn't just pack a bag and go; you'd plan your stops, budget for meals, and maybe even splurge on a few luxuries. That's what we're doing here but for your retirement.

Understanding Your Lifestyle Choices

Your retirement lifestyle is the big kahuna in this equation. It's all about how you want to spend your days once the white coat is hung up for good.

- **Day-to-Day Living:** Consider your current expenses. Will they go up or down? Most folks find healthcare costs creep up while commuting costs might vanish.

- **Dream Vacations:** Got a bucket list? Those dream trips aren't going to fund themselves. Factor in a few big adventures in the early years of retirement.

- **Hobbies and Pastimes:** Picking up golf? Planning to paint? Hobbies can be a significant part of your retirement budget.

- **Home Sweet Home:** Planning to downsize or finally snag that beachfront property? Where you live affects your cost of living big time.

- **Giving Back:** Many retirees find joy in donating to causes close to their heart. If that sounds like you, make sure to budget for generosity.

Inflation's Impact

Inflation is the sneaky little bugger that can eat away at your savings without you even noticing. It's the reason a movie ticket won't cost the same in 20 years as it does now.

- **Yearly Increases:** Historically, inflation averages about 3% per year. This means you'll need more money each year just to maintain the same lifestyle.

- **Healthcare Costs:** These tend to rise faster than general inflation. If healthcare costs increase by 5% annually, your budget needs to keep pace.

- **Cost of Living Adjustments:** Some of your retirement income, like Social Security, might adjust for inflation, but don't count on all your income sources to do so.

- **Long-Term Planning:** Over 20 or 30 years, inflation can drastically reduce your purchasing power. Planning for this is non-negotiable.

- **Safe Withdrawal Rates:** Factor in inflation when you calculate how much you can safely withdraw from your savings each year.

Future Healthcare Needs

Healthcare is a biggie, especially as we age. It's probably going to be one of your biggest expenses in retirement, so let's give it the attention it deserves.

- **Medicare and Beyond:** Medicare covers a lot, but not everything. Budget for premiums, co-pays, and things Medicare doesn't cover, like most dental work.

- **Long-Term Care:** Nobody likes to think about it, but there's a chance you might need some form of long-term care. It's pricey, so planning ahead is key.

- **Health Savings Accounts (HSAs):** If you have an HSA, it can be a godsend for tax-free healthcare spending in retirement.

- **Out-of-Pocket Costs:** Even with insurance, expect some out-of-pocket costs. Glasses, hearing aids, and other gadgets can add up.

- **Healthy Living**: Investing in your health now can pay off big time later. It's not just good for you; it's good for your wallet, too.

By breaking down these aspects of your retirement needs, you're setting yourself up for a much smoother ride. Sure, it takes a bit of legwork now, but think of it as investing in your future happiness. Retirement is your time to shine, so let's make sure you've got the resources to do it in style.

8.2 The Path to Financial Independence

Financial independence sounds like a lofty goal, but it's totally doable with the right plan. First off, know where you stand. Surprisingly, only 48% of doctors feel on track for a comfy retirement. Let's not be part of that stat. Start with maxing out retirement accounts - 401(k)s, IRAs, you name it. And here's a pro tip: don't overlook health savings accounts (HSAs). They're like a stealth retirement account with triple tax advantages. Aim to save at least 15-20% of your income, but more is better. It's like packing extra snacks for a long hike; you'll thank yourself later.

Following Diverse Income Streams

When we talk about building wealth, it's like setting up a buffet of income sources. You don't want to rely just on your day job, right? That's where side hustles come into play. And for doctors, this could mean anything from consulting to medical writing. The key is to find something you're passionate about, so it doesn't feel like work. Every extra dollar you earn is another dollar you can invest towards your financial freedom.

Well, with income, it's spot on. Think about it: if your main job is your only income and something goes sideways, you're in a pickle. But if you've got a side hustle or two, it's like having a safety net. And the cool part? More than a third of folks out there are doing just this, padding their wallets with extra cash from side gigs.

Now, consider this: side hustles aren't just about making extra dough; they're about exploring passions you might not get to in your day job. Love teaching? Tutoring on the side can be both fulfilling and profitable. Into writing? Medical blogging or freelance writing can open new doors. It's all about mixing business with pleasure.

Here's a nugget of wisdom: your side hustle can also be a smart way to test the waters for a potential career pivot or retirement gig. It's like a low-risk trial run for what could become a major income stream down the line. And who knows? It might just grow into something big.

Think about the power of passive income, too. It's money that keeps coming in, even when you're not actively working for it. Rental properties, dividend stocks, or even creating an online course can set you up for some sweet, ongoing cash flow. And the best part? It can give you a bit of financial breathing room to take bigger risks or make more aggressive investments elsewhere.

Lastly, remember that every side hustle or passive income stream you set up is also a chance to learn new skills and expand your network. It's not just about the extra cash; it's about growing personally and professionally. And in the grand scheme of your financial independence journey, those experiences can be just as valuable as the income they bring in.

Investing Wisely

Now, let's chat about making your money work for you. Investing can sound daunting, but it doesn't have to be. Start with the basics: stocks, bonds, and maybe some real estate. It's all about balance. A well-diversified portfolio can reduce your risk and smooth out the bumps along the road. Think of it as a safety net for your financial future. And with technology today, getting started is easier than ever. There are apps and platforms that can guide you through the process, even if you're not a Wall Street whiz.

- **Start with the Basics:** You know, getting into investing doesn't mean you have to jump into complex stuff right off the bat. It's like learning to swim; you don't dive into the deep end without knowing the strokes. Stocks and bonds are your swimming lessons here. Did you know that historically, the stock market has returned about 10% annually? That's a solid start for growing your wealth.

- **Keep Costs Low:** Ever noticed how fees can sneak up on you? Whether it's that extra charge for guac or investment fees, they add up. When you're picking investments, look for low-cost options like index funds. Warren Buffett, ever heard of him? He's a big fan of them for a reason. They mirror the market's performance, so you're riding the wave without those pesky high fees eating into your returns.

- **Diversify, Diversify, Diversify:** Can't stress this enough. Putting all your money in one stock is like betting everything on a single card hand. Spread your investments across different sectors and asset classes. It's your safety net. If one part dips, you're not going belly up. A mix of stocks, bonds, and maybe some real estate can give your portfolio the balance it needs.

- **Think Long-Term:** Remember, investing is a marathon, not a sprint. Those stories of people making a quick buck? They're more about luck than strategy. Real wealth building takes time. It's about sticking to your plan, even when the market gets bumpy. Over 20 years, the S&P 500 has returned about 6% per year, even including the downturns. Patience pays.

Stay Informed but Don't Overdo It: Keeping an eye on your investments is smart, but overchecking can lead you to make hasty decisions. It's like baking a cake; you don't keep opening the oven every two minutes. The market will have its ups and downs, but if your investments are solid and well-researched, they'll likely grow over time.
Set regular check-ins for your portfolio, maybe quarterly or bi-annually, so you're informed but not impulsive.

For example, stocks and bonds are generally uncorrelated. When stocks go down, it is helpful if bonds go up to give you some protection. However, correlations are always changing and can often throw some unexpected curveballs.

In 2022, something unusual happened – both stocks and bonds went down at the same time. It's not something we see often, but experts think it might happen more often in the future. A big hedge fund, AQR, mentioned that we might see something like what happened back in the 70s, 80s, and 90s, where stocks and bonds move together, especially if inflation keeps being unpredictable.

Then, in August 2023, I saw this headline on Bloomberg that really caught my eye: "Bonds are a useless hedge for stock losses as correlation jumps." It was saying that the way stocks and bonds usually balance each other out wasn't working like it used to. In fact, they were moving together more than they had since 1996!

This is super important for us to think about when we're planning how to invest our money. It means the old rules might not always apply, and we need to be smart about spreading our investments into different things, not just stocks and bonds. It's all about staying flexible and keeping an eye on how things are changing so we can make the best moves for our money.

Mastering Money Management

Here's the thing: earning money is one part of the equation, but managing it? That's where the real magic happens. Budgeting might not sound sexy, but it's your secret weapon for financial independence. It's about knowing where your money's going and making sure you're saving enough to meet your goals. And yes, that includes fun money for now because enjoying the journey is just as important as the destination. So, get cozy with your budget, and watch your path to financial independence become clearer with each smart decision you make.

- **Setting Up Savings on Autopilot:** You know how we set reminders for everything these days, from patient appointments to grabbing groceries? Why not do the same with saving? By automating your savings, it's like you're telling your money, "Hey, go take care of my future self, will ya?" Before you know it, you've got a growing stash without even thinking about it. It's a no-brainer, really.

- **Trimming the Fat on Spending:** Ever looked at your bank statement and thought, "Where did all my money go?" Happens to the best of us. But here's a little nudge: scrutinize those statements like you would a patient's chart. Do you really need that super deluxe cable package or that gym membership you barely use? Cutting back on these can feel like a mini pay raise, seriously. Redirect that cash into your savings, and you're golden.

- **Getting a Money Mentor:** Ever consider that maybe you don't have to go at this alone? Just like in medicine, having a mentor can make a world of difference. A wealth strategist isn't just for the ultra-rich; they're for anyone who wants to get their money's worth, literally. They can help you dodge financial pitfalls and keep you on track for that early retirement dream. It's like having a personal trainer, but for your wallet.

8.3 Sustainable Withdrawal Strategies

Alright, you've made it to retirement - high five! Now, how do you make sure your money lasts as long as you do? Enter the 4% rule. It's like the golden rule of retirement spending. Basically, you can safely withdraw 4% of your nest egg in the first year of retirement, then adjust for inflation after that. But remember, this rule isn't one-size-fits-all. With medical advances pushing life expectancy upwards (hello, 90s and beyond!), considering a more conservative 3% could be your ticket to a worry-free retirement. And always, always have a rainy-day fund for those unexpected health hiccups or market mood swings.

Flexibility Is Key

Now, sticking strictly to the 4% (or 3%) rule is smart, but life's not always a straight line, right? Some years, the market's up, and you're feeling like a Wall Street whiz. Other times, not so much. That's where a bit of flexibility can be a game-changer. Think of your withdrawal rate as a speed limit. Sure, 4% is the signposted limit, but if you hit a patch of bad weather (hello, market downturn), slowing down a bit won't hurt. In fact, studies show that folks who adjust their withdrawals based on market performance can significantly decrease the risk of running out of dough. So, if the market takes a nosedive, consider tightening the belt for a bit. On the flip side, if things are looking rosy, you might grab a little extra for that dream vacation.

- **Annual Review Ritual:** Make it a habit, like your annual health check-up. Once a year, sit down with your financial statements and take a good look at how your investments are doing. If the market's been good to you, maybe you can afford to splurge a bit more on those hobbies or trips you've been eyeing. On the flip side, if things are looking tight, it might be time to trim the sails and cut back on non-essential spending. This isn't just about numbers; it's about ensuring your financial plan stays in sync with your life and the ever-changing economic landscape.

- **Spending Guardrails:** Think of these as your financial speed bumps. Set up upper and lower spending limits based on your withdrawal rate. For instance, if you've decided on a 4% withdrawal rate, you might set your guardrails at 3.5% and 4.5%. If your spending starts creeping up beyond your upper limit, it's a signal to ease back. Conversely, if you're well under your lower limit, you might have a little wiggle room for some extra indulgences. This approach gives you a clear framework for adjusting your spending while keeping your long-term plan on track.

- **Tax-Smart Withdrawals:** Taxes can take a big bite out of your retirement savings if you're not careful. Be smart about which accounts you withdraw from and when. For example, pulling from your Roth IRA (where withdrawals are tax-free) might make more sense in a year when you're already facing a high tax bill. On the other hand, tapping into taxable accounts or traditional IRAs (which are taxed as income) might be more advantageous in lower-income years. Mixing and matching withdrawals can help you manage your tax bracket and keep more money in your pocket.

- **Market Downturn Strategies:** When the market takes a hit, it's tempting to panic and pull back on all spending. But there's a middle ground. Focus on cutting discretionary spending while preserving what's essential for your happiness and well-being. Maybe you postpone that big trip or dine out less often, but you keep funding those hobbies or activities that bring you the most joy. It's about making thoughtful choices that balance financial prudence with life satisfaction.

- **Dynamic Spending Models:** Some retirees swear by more sophisticated models that adjust withdrawals based on market performance. For example, you might start with a 4% withdrawal rate but allow for a 5% increase after a year when your investments grow by more than 10%. Conversely, you'd scale back after a down year. These models can get pretty complex, but the basic idea is to let your spending ebb and flow with the tides of the market, keeping your retirement finances resilient in the face of uncertainty.

Following flexibility in your withdrawal strategy is like having a good pair of shock absorbers on your car. It makes the ride smoother, no matter what bumps the road might throw your way.

The Bucket Strategy

Now, for a strategy that's as cool as it sounds: the Bucket Strategy. Picture your retirement savings split into a few different "buckets," each with its own purpose and timeline. The first bucket is for the short term, filled with super-safe investments like cash or short-term bonds. This is your go-to for the first few years of retirement, so no heart palpitations every time the stock market sneezes.

The second bucket? That's your medium-term fund. Think of it as a buffer zone, stocked with a mix of slightly riskier assets like intermediate bonds or dividend-paying stocks. This bucket is there to refill your short-term bucket as you dip into it over the years.

And the third bucket, that's where the fun is. It's your long-term growth engine, chock-full of stocks and other assets with the potential for higher returns. You won't touch this for a while, so it's got time to grow and weather the market's ups and downs.

This setup gives you the perfect blend of security and growth potential. When the markets are up, you can top up your buckets from the growth bucket. And when things look grim, you've got your short-term reserves to lean on without having to sell your investments at a loss. It's like having a financial safety net, so you can enjoy those retirement years without sweating the small stuff.

Conclusion: Setting Sail for Early Retirement

As we wrap up this chapter on envisioning early retirement, remember that the journey to hanging up your white coat ahead of time is as much about smart planning as it is about dreaming big. Calculating your retirement needs, forging a path to financial independence, and strategizing sustainable withdrawals are your navigational tools for this adventure. Think of it as charting your course through uncharted waters, with the stars of your goals to guide you.

But retirement isn't just about reaching a destination; it's about what you do when you get there. As we segue into Chapter 9, we'll explore how to ensure your wealth doesn't just last but leaves a lasting impact. It's about turning your financial success into a legacy that resonates beyond the bounds of your own life, enriching the lives of others, and crafting a story that will be told for generations.

So, as you set your sights on early retirement, remember that it's just the beginning of a new, exciting chapter. Stay tuned for how to make this next phase of life not only fulfilling for you but beneficial for the world you'll leave behind. Let's turn the page together and discover how to craft a legacy that lasts.

Chapter 9: Leaving a Legacy

Well, here we are at the final chapter of our journey together. It's been quite the ride, hasn't it? We've navigated the highs and lows of financial planning, from tackling that mountain of debt to designing a life that lets you hang up your white coat sooner than you ever dreamed possible. Now, it's time to zoom out and look at the bigger picture: the legacy you'll leave behind.

In this chapter, we're going to explore three powerful ways to cement your legacy. First up, we'll dive into how your success can fuel philanthropic efforts and make a tangible impact on the world. Next, we'll decode the nuts and bolts of setting up trusts, foundations, and other vehicles to ensure your legacy lasts for generations. And finally, we'll talk about something close to home—educating your family about financial responsibility and the value of giving back.

9.1 Philanthropy as a Legacy

So, you've worked hard, saved diligently, and now you're thinking, "What's next?" It's not just about what you leave behind; it's about the mark you make. Take Dr. Smith, for example (not his real name, but bare with me). After a rewarding career, he started a clinic in an underserved area, changing countless lives. It's incredible, right? And get this: around 20% of doctors are actively involved in charitable work outside their practice. You could be one of them, using your success to fuel change and make a real impact.

My dad, who has an internal medicine background, spends half the year at a free clinic in Lahore, Pakistan. For me? I like to build schools. Check out one of our training sites we recently made and see how peoples faces are lighting up!

Let's break it down into how you can really make a splash with your giving, in a way that feels right and does a whole lot of good.

The Ripple Effect of Giving

So, you've decided to give back. Awesome! But here's the cool part: the impact of your giving goes way beyond just the check you write. It's like when you drop a single pebble in a pond, and those ripples just keep spreading out. For example, if you help fund a local clinic, it's not just the patients who benefit. Their families are healthier, kids can go to school instead of staying home sick, and parents can work without worrying. Here's a quick rundown:

- **Better Health:** A clinic you help fund could significantly lower illness rates in the area.

- **Smarter Kids:** Scholarships or school supplies can mean more kids hitting the books and less hitting dead ends.

- **Stronger Economy:** Healthier, educated folks contribute to the local economy, making the whole community more vibrant.

- **Inspiration Station:** Seeing your good deeds might just inspire your doctor buddies to start their own giving.

- **Feel-Good Vibes:** Don't forget, giving back feels amazing. There's no matching that warm, fuzzy feeling you get.

Building a Philanthropic Strategy

Alright, wanting to help is one thing, but making a real difference? That takes some planning. Say you're all about education. Focusing your giving on things like scholarships means every dollar you donate is doing exactly what you want it to do. Here's how you can get strategic:

- **Find Your Fire:** Pinpoint what gets you fired up. Is it education? Healthcare? Clean water? Start there.

- **Team Up:** Look for groups already doing great work in your area of interest. Joining forces can make your contribution go even further.

- **Think Long-Term:** How can you keep the support going? Maybe it's setting aside a bit of your income regularly.

- **Bring Friends:** Get your circle involved. More hands on deck mean more good work getting done.

- **Track Your Impact:** Keep an eye on how your contributions are making waves. It's okay to tweak your plan to up your impact.

Legacy Through Philanthropy

Here's where it gets really personal. Your giving isn't just about the money; it's about leaving a piece of yourself with the world, a legacy that says, "I was here, and I helped." Whether that's a scholarship in your name, a program you kickstart, or a cause you champion, it's all about making a lasting impact. Keep these thoughts in mind:

- **Make It Stick:** Aim for contributions that keep on giving, long into the future.

- **Personal Touch:** Tie your giving to something that means a lot to you personally. It makes it that much more special.

- **Family Affair:** Get your family in on the action. Passing down the value of giving is a legacy in itself.

- **Be Seen:** While it's not about the spotlight, being open about your philanthropy can encourage others to step up too.

- **Stay Flexible:** Be open to shifting your focus as you learn what works best and where the need is greatest.

So, there you have it. Philanthropy isn't just about writing checks. It's about using what you've got to make a real difference, in a way that feels true to who you are and what you believe in. What better legacy is there than that?

9.2 Structuring a Lasting Legacy

Now, let's talk brass tacks about making sure your legacy stands the test of time. Trusts, foundations, you name it—these aren't just for the ultra-wealthy. They're tools that can help you pass on not just your wealth, but your values. For instance, setting up a scholarship fund in your name at your alma mater could inspire future generations of healers. And did you know that by properly setting up a trust, you could also ensure that your financial help reaches your loved ones exactly when they need it most?

Diving deeper into the idea of creating a lasting legacy, It's like building a bridge. You might not always be the one to cross it, but you know it will help others reach new places and create connections for years to come.. When we talk about setting up trusts or foundations, it's not just about the legal mumbo jumbo. It's really about planting those seeds for the future. For instance, did you know that by setting up a charitable trust, you're not just giving away money? You're actually setting up a whole system that keeps on giving, based on your initial input. It's kind of like setting up a domino effect where your one act of kindness keeps rolling forward.

And here's the thing about making your legacy resonate—it doesn't have to be a grand gesture. Small pebbles make big ripples. Say you're passionate about education; even a small scholarship fund can make a huge difference. It's about giving someone a leg up, just like you might have had, or wished you had, at some point. And the stats back this up—over 80% of donations come from individuals, just like you and me, not big corporations. That's a lot of people making a lot of little ripples that all add up to a big wave of change.

So, when you're thinking about your legacy, think about what matters the most to you. What's your 'why'? And remember, it's not just about the dollars and cents. It's about the values you want to pass on. Maybe you write a letter to go with your will, something that tells your story and the values you held dear. It's these personal touches that turn a financial gesture into a meaningful legacy. It's about making sure that your story, your lessons, and your values live on, touching lives and making a difference in ways that matter long after you're gone.

To sum it up, here are a few key takeaways to consider when structuring your lasting legacy:

- **Flexibility is Key:** Trusts can be tailored to meet specific needs, whether it's funding education, supporting charitable causes, or providing for family members with special needs.

- **Align with Your Passions:** Use your legacy to support causes or initiatives that are close to your heart, ensuring your impact is both meaningful and personal.

- **Consider the Ripple Effect:** Understand that your contributions can inspire change and innovation, filling crucial gaps in funding and support.

- **Personal Touch Matters:** Beyond financial assets, consider leaving a legacy letter to impart your values, experiences, and hopes for future generations.

- **Engage with Professionals:** Collaborating with wealth strategist and legal professionals can help ensure your legacy is structured effectively and in accordance with your wishes.

Remember, structuring a lasting legacy is a deeply personal journey. It's about crafting a narrative that not only reflects your life's work but also ignites progress and inspiration long into the future. What story do you want to tell?

9.3 Family and Financial Education

Last but not least, let's not forget the home front. Teaching your kids or grandkids about money isn't just about piggy banks or lemonade stands. It's about instilling values that can last a lifetime. Consider this: a study found that kids who discussed finances with their parents were more likely to save and budget wisely as adults. So, why not start a family tradition of giving, or involve them in decisions about supporting causes? It's about passing on a legacy of generosity and wisdom, one conversation at a time.

Diving deeper into "Family and Financial Education," it's all about making those crucial conversations around money as natural as discussing weekend plans. Think about the ripple effect of discussing something as simple as grocery shopping choices or comparing prices before a purchase. It's not just about saving a few dollars here and there; it's about instilling a mindset that values thoughtful decision-making. And the impact? Well, studies suggest that engaging kids in budgeting and financial planning activities can boost their financial literacy by up to 30%. That's setting them up for a future where they're not just surviving but thriving.

Now, let's talk role models. Ever noticed how kids often mimic what they see? When they observe you juggling bills, making savings a priority, or even setting aside a charity fund, they're picking up more than just good habits. They're learning about priorities, empathy, and the balance between wants and needs. It's like those moments when you catch them pretending to be 'the adult'—it's cute, but it's also them processing and practicing the world around them. So, when you involve them in financial decisions, explaining why you chose one investment over another or why saving for college is critical, you're essentially giving them a masterclass in real-life financial management, far more valuable than any textbook lesson.

But let's not sugarcoat it—money talks can get tricky, especially when budgets are tight or financial goals seem like mountains too high to climb. Yet, it's in these challenging conversations that some of the most valuable lessons are learned. It's about showing resilience in the face of setbacks, the importance of adjusting sails when the wind changes direction, and the power of teamwork in overcoming obstacles. A survey revealed that families who openly discuss financial challenges and work together to find solutions report a stronger bond and mutual respect among members. It's about fostering an environment where it's okay to ask questions, express concerns, and even offer suggestions. This inclusive approach doesn't just empower each family member; it strengthens the family unit, making it a formidable team ready to take on the world, one financial decision at a time

Here are five points to keep in mind when fostering family and financial education:

- **Start Early and Keep it Age-Appropriate:** Tailor your financial lessons to match your child's age and understanding. For the little ones, it might be as simple as a piggy bank; for teens, it could mean managing a small weekly budget.

- **Set Family Financial Goals Together:** Whether it's saving for a vacation or a new family car, setting shared goals can turn financial planning into a team effort.

- **Encourage Earning and Saving:** Support them in starting a mini-business or doing chores for an allowance, highlighting the satisfaction of earning and saving towards something special.

- **Be Transparent About Household Finances:** Without overwhelming them, share some basics of your household budgeting. It helps demystify finances and shows them the real-world implications of financial decisions.

- **Celebrate Financial Milestones:** Just like any other achievement, celebrate when financial goals are met. It reinforces positive behavior and shows that financial responsibility is valued and rewarded in your family.

By integrating these principles into your family life, you're not just teaching your kids about money; you're equipping them with the tools to build a secure, informed, and responsible financial future.

Conclusion

As we wrap up our journey through the pages of this book, it's clear that the path to financial independence and early retirement for doctors is paved with more than just good intentions. It's built on the bedrock of sound financial practices, a deep understanding of personal and professional priorities, and the courage to make bold decisions when it counts. We've navigated the complexities of debt management, investment strategies, and the importance of a well-rounded approach to wealth that includes not just financial gain, but also personal fulfillment and a lasting legacy.

Remember, every chapter you've read is a stepping stone towards a future where financial worries won't dictate your life choices. A future where you'll be free to pursue your passions, both within and beyond the medical field, without the shadow of financial constraints looming over you. It's about more than just retiring early; it's about living fully.

But as we close this chapter, remember that the journey doesn't end here. The world of finance is ever-evolving, and staying informed is key to maintaining and growing your wealth. As the famous investor Warren Buffett once said, "The more you learn, the more you earn." Let that be a guiding principle as you move forward.

If you're ready to take the next step in securing your financial future and exploring the possibilities that early retirement can offer, I invite you to reach out to Baluch Capital, we're dedicated to helping medical professionals like you navigate the intricacies of investment and wealth management, tailored to the unique challenges and opportunities of your profession.

Together, let's chart a course towards a future rich in both wealth and life's joys. Your journey to financial enlightenment and freedom is just beginning, and Baluch Capital is here to guide you every step of the way.

Epilogue: The Renaissance Never Ends

Continued Learning and Growth

So, we've journeyed together through the ins and outs of securing a financial future that lets you hang up your white coat early if you choose. But here's the thing: the world of finance, much like medicine, never stands still. It's always evolving, always throwing new challenges and opportunities our way.

Think about it—just a couple of decades ago, who would have thought we'd be trading stocks from our phones or investing in digital currencies? That's why it's crucial to stay curious, to keep learning. Did you know that a staggering 73% of wealthy individuals attribute their continued success to their habit of never stopping learning? That's right. The learning never stops, and neither should we.

The Community of Financially Savvy Physicians

Now, let's talk about the power of community. Going at it alone can be tough, no matter how strong or smart you are. But when you're part of a community, especially one that shares your unique challenges and goals, the journey becomes a whole lot easier—and a lot more fun.

Consider this: studies show that people who share their goals and progress with a supportive community are significantly more likely to achieve their aims. It's not just about swapping tips and tricks; it's about building each other up, sharing successes and setbacks, and sometimes, just knowing you're not alone in your aspirations.

So, what do you say? Let's keep the conversation going. Join a forum, attend a webinar, or maybe even start a small group with some colleagues. Whatever shape it takes, being part of a community of financially savvy physicians can be one of the most rewarding aspects of this journey.

Appendices: The Renaissance Toolkit

Resources for Financial Education

Let's dive into some gold mines of financial wisdom. I've curated a list of must-reads and must-dos that'll turn you into a finance whiz in no time. We're talking about books that break down complex concepts into bite-sized, easy-to-digest pieces. Think of them as your financial cheat codes. And courses? Some out there can transform you from a finance newbie to a savvy investor, all from the comfort of your couch. Plus, don't overlook online platforms. They're like virtual libraries brimming with knowledge, ready to be explored. Around 60% of successful investors swear by continuous learning as their secret sauce. So, let's get you in on that action.

Tools for Financial Management

Next up, let's gear you up with some nifty tools. Budgeting might sound as fun as watching paint dry, but hear me out. With the right app or spreadsheet, it can be as easy as pie. And we're not stopping at budgeting. I'm talking about investment trackers that make keeping an eye on your portfolio a breeze, and goal-setting templates that keep you on track like a GPS for your finances. Did you know that people who use financial management tools are 33% more likely to feel confident about their financial future? Let's get you into that confident crew.

www.ingramcontent.com/pod-product-compliance
Lightning Source LLC
Chambersburg PA
CBHW071833210526
45479CB00001B/115